Endorsements

Thumper Jordan Nagasako, the Author's Son: "I was very lucky to grow up as a homeschooler. I feel it's more accurate to say I grew up with life or "the real world" as my school. The mentality that I have gained from my upbringing has made a huge difference in my thought processes. Starting with an unschooling approach let my natural drive flourish and gave me the freedom to choose formal lessons when I was ready. Most of my fellow homeschooled peers are not only very genuine people but also efficient, self-driven individuals who look at education as something you do throughout your whole life, not something you did and got done with.

"I would like to thank my parents for their support and trust of who I am. They nurtured me to become my own person. I look back on my happy childhood and education as a family-oriented lifestyle that I hope to some day provide for my children."

Lawrence Koss, M.Ed: "As a former public school teacher privileged to know the author and witness the fruits of what she writes, I can attest to her son having grown into a remarkable young man. He is self-directed yet able to work well in a team, creative, adventurous, bright, caring, responsible, and quite successful as an athlete and entrepreneur. What I like most about Gail's book is that in an easy-to-read, "down-home" fashion, everything a prospective home school parent needs is right here. In my opinion, were one to consider home schooling and wish to talk with someone who did it in a relaxed, informative, encouraging fashion ... one need go no further than this book."

Geralyn Doskoch, M.D., family physician: "There is nothing more paramount than the physical and emotional well-being of our children. Homeschooling offers a means to accomplish raising competent, caring individuals, but to many families the task can seem daunting. In this practical how-to guide, Gail Nagasako brings a wealth of professional knowledge and personal experience to take the fear out of taking this step. For anybody considering homeschooling but not sure where to start – this is the place!"

Naomi Aldort, Ph.D, Author, *Raising Our Children, Raising Ourselves:* "Many parents are dissatisfied with school but have not considered homeschooling because they see it as difficult or are afraid it wouldn't meet the educational or social needs of their children. Ms. Nagasako debunks these myths, revealing the educational and social advantages of learning outside of school and providing clear and accessible guidance to making the transition."

Elizabeth Wertheim, B.A. founder and director of Rivendell and Maui Sudbury alternative schools: "Gail is a long time friend. We have worked together on various family and unschooling related projects. Gail has a very fine tuned ability to listen compassionately to each person she is with and thus be able to reflect back what is needed for them in order to find their own answers and/or solutions to life's ever present challenges. She brings this talent to her interactions with homeschoolers and their parents. I am thrilled that she is now masterfully and magically sharing the fruits of her labors with you and your learning community."

Helen Hegener, editor, Home Education Magazine: "Gail has written for us over the years and her insights and clear style are well regarded by our readers. "

Lesley Alexander, M.Ed, District Educational Specialist, Hawaii Department of Education: "Every parent must decide how to best educate their children. This is a very private and personal decision. It is a decision that will affect the quality of children's lives through their impressionable elementary years, to the labyrinth of adolescence and certainly into adulthood, playing a role in determining their choices for further schooling, career options, and even marriage.

"Gail Nagasako has lived, researched and written an excellent guide for parents wanting to explore the unique choice to home-school. Read this guide well; you will find that if the decision to home school rings true for you, your family and especially for the unique needs of your children, that there is ample research to support your decision and your children can achieve every bit as well and possibly even better than children matriculating from quality private and public education systems.

"When homeschooling is done right, the DOE never sees those kids again, or they return so easily that they do not hit "the radar" so to speak. It is when it is done poorly that the DOE is alerted and therefore there has become a bias in

DOE that homeschooling does not work. I know it does from my personal experience of friends and from research – but I also am aware of it when it does not.

"Too often we find children whose parents have not given homeschooling the attention it requires and those children have suffered as a result. Parents who choose to home-school will find this book a real help in ensuring the success of their children academically and socially."

Homeschooling
Why and How

Homeschooling

Why and How

Gail Nagasako

Two Harbors Press
Minneapolis, MN

Two Harbors Press
212 3rd Avenue North, Suite 290
Minneapolis, MN 55401
612.455.2293
www.TwoHarborsPress.com

ISBN-13: 978-1-937293-46-8
LCCN: 2011939429

Distributed by Itasca Books

Cover Design and Typeset by Sophie Chi

Printed in the United States of America

Testimonials

Thank you for your time and again, I love your book. I found it so helpful especially when I wrote down the answers to the three questions about what I am good at, what I am not good at and things I don't like.

I have decided to homeschool (5 year old) Kade myself, and not follow any particular curriculum. Life is the best teacher. We have already started teaching Kade about money. Gabe has offered to Kade a business opportunity helping him with a recycling business that Kade wants to call "Kade's recycling". Gabe told him that he would make chicken wire baskets and put a sign on it for "Kade's recycling" and he will take Kade on Wednesday and Saturday to go and pick up the bottles in the bins and recycle them. We want to put them at our families' houses who don't recycle and at some businesses. He's so excited at the fact that he will be making more money in addition to his "family pay".

Krystal M.

Thanks for fighting this battle for us, generations after generations will read it and be so grateful you were born before them. I remember getting mad at Charito and my son because of homework and how they will look down or even cry, now they will hug me and tell me they love me about 3 or more times a day. We owe you big time!! If you need me to clean your car or do grocery shopping just let me know!! I love the 64 reason why we home school!

(a few weeks later) My son gave me 2 big hugs while I was brushing my teeth, then caught me in the hallway, hugged me again and said " this is because I love you too much" I have been reading about "unschooling" and it's like winning the lottery! I love the freedom!

Take care please,

Aileen S.

I wasn't worried about the academic requirements of homeschooling. My nagging doubt was that I was depriving my children of experiences they should be having in school. When I read Gail's '64 Reasons Why We Homeschool', my doubts were totally put to rest. It's amazing what loving and wise words can do. My confidence soared after reading Gail's list. I am so glad we continued with homeschooling. It's the best decision we ever made."

Sonia S, Washington

It was no accident that as I was reading your homeschool guide that I met Otto and Melisa who happen to be your friends from homeschooling. I really enjoyed your information and made me feel confident in my homeschooling choice. I have two boys, Luke (eight) and Logan (six) whom I homeschool. We have been using the K12 curriculum through the charter school for three years now. It is nice because it gives us some structure while at the same time allowing me the flexibility to let the boys develop at their own pace with some days simply building Lego's and making up stories with their creations. I would love to talk to you sometime on the phone as reading your book has given me a boast of energy.

Tim J.

My son, Chris, adores Thumper. We were watching him practice yesterday. (Did not know he was your son until I looked up homeschooling information in Hawaii)
Again, Mahalo!

Peggylee F. S

Thanks for your help, after reading what you have on the website I became very encouraged and interested in considering homeschooling. My husband feels it's the best way to go, I kept making excuses because I'm afraid of being responsible for my son's failure and his future.

Carolyn R

Thank you for sharing all your knowledge, trials, and success. Reading your information helped me to realize that my child and I can succeed..... We have struggled with public schools since preschool, but have never encountered the problems we have had at (___) middle school. Last night my husband and I resolved that we would no longer subject our son to that environment.

Janet D.

INCREDIBLE absolutely INCREDIBLE. I just read your "Bodyboarding and Rollerblading Curriculum." That is exactly what I want to do with Logan. Not necessarily body boarding or rollerblading, but just yesterday he was telling me how he wishes he could skateboard better. Wow. We are going to the skate park today after school.

One step at a time, it usually takes me some time for things to kick in.... So, now to be directed in this manner towards home schooling or even better unschooling blows my mind.

I am soooooo fortunate to have met you thru my doula work with Jennifer. The powers that be really do work in beautifully mysterious ways, don't they?

Thank you for all the information and contacts. –
Love,

Mary Jane

I came across Gail Nagasako on-line when researching for more information on homeschooling. I found her writing to be easy-going, understandable, informational and most of all helpful. What most impressed me was her willingness to help others. I wrote her an email and was surprised and happy to have received a reply from her right away. She truly is a great resource to have. I feel more prepared and quite excited to take the jump into homeschooling.

Alissa P.

Your advice brought peace to my spirit. — **A mother**

Gail, I wanted to tell you it did NOT take me this long to read your book; it's just that reading your book was so momentous that it created a beautiful shift in our family. We've been pretty busy implementing big changes and it's partially because of you! Actually, it's kind of like the straw that broke the camel's proverbial back. I've been thinking about this actively for two years, finally got the courage to do it! It was a great opportunity for me to read yet another homeschooling book (my seventh), and yours was so powerful and accessible that it seemed to be the catalyst for change. This week, I filed my private school affidavit and today was my daughter's last day in the public school system. We're free!!!! Thank you so much for sending the manuscript to me; I feel privileged to have been one of its earliest readers. Your advice was straightforward and very helpful. I especially loved all of the great quotes from great thinkers throughout our time on education and learning. One of the things that touched me most was the way you described the spectrum of homeschoolers, from the boxed curriculum schedule keepers, to religious people, to radical unschoolers. This also gave me strength to do what I truly believe will be right for our family. Instead of taking this journey and starting out in the middle of the spectrum somewhere and buying a curriculum and trying to make my beautiful ADD girl keep to a schedule, I've decided to take the leap and trust her individual learning style. I'm going to unschool (well, first I'm actually going to deschool because we had a rough road there for a while and we need to decompress!), and eventually do child-directed learning. I'm excited because SHE is excited too. She thinks it is extremely "cool" that she can do math in her pajamas. I am going to continue to focus on her music studies first and foremost, and then let the rest of it flow from there naturally.

Thank you again for sharing with us, you've made all the

difference in the world! I hope we keep in touch.

(and added a week or so later)

I know I said too much in my last email, but after reading this I can't help myself. I have to say one more thing. If you do put my words in your book, great! But also can you add one thing: and this is really important. It's something I'm just beginning to get to the heart of. Unschooling is NOT just an educational philosophy; it is a LIFE philosophy. It is changing both me and my daughter at the same time. All that you said about discovery is the key to it. How many adults do you know that really WANT to explore, learn, research, read, figure out new things? They've been negatively programmed by many years of traditional schooling to be revolted by the thought of going back to school. It scares them. Who could blame them? Who would want to take that on again? But when you are free to explore the world in all its facets, scientific, literary, you name it, and do so at your own pace, you really begin to slowly redevelop that inherent love of learning. It's what separates us from the other mammals really. The act of learning and thus the act of creation (music is a great example of this). It's very difficult to learn music theory, but it is essential to music writing. And yet we are the only mammals who do this. But haven't you found most musicians to be "outside the box" – somehow they got through the traditional educational system and meanwhile forged this personal musical path. It is the essence of loving something that is challenging, being a musician or composer. That's how I'm looking at unschooling. It's a life plan, not just a way to teach the three R's. This is so important to not just how to approach unschooling a child (who is a free and independent little PERSON!), but how to approach our own continuing adult education and LIFE!

I hope that makes sense to readers. It's SO important. It's so inspiring. This sounds silly, but it kind of makes me well up inside. *Tokeli*

Dedication

To all the parents with the courage
to question what *is*
And the vision to seek *what could be*
For the sake of their children.

Author and son happily begin their journey.

Contents

Chapter 3: What's Next?

A homeschool whale watch field trip

Preface

Despite all the attempts at reform and an enormous budget, students in American schools keep falling behind other countries in rankings. Socialization in some of these institutions has become so dysfunctional that many schools have resorted to installing metal detectors to protect students from one another. Teachers and students sometimes have to submit to random drug testing to deal with the problem of drugs in schools. Buildings and materials suffer for lack of funds. Underpaid teachers struggle with larger class sizes, and more intrusive government testing requirements leave little time for creative lessons. Your children's school may be an exception, but even the best schools have their own problems.

Until recently, it seemed our only options were to struggle within the system or to send our children to expensive private schools in hopes they could do better. My intention in writing this book is to help you see other options and to help you feel empowered to choose the path that is best for your family. I am making no attempt here to sell you on homeschooling or to tell you everything there is to know about it, as that is not at all necessary or even desirable. Instead, I aim to give you a briefing on the reasons to homeschool and enough information for you to know what it involves, whether it's something you want to try, and how you can do it. It really is easier than you think.

A decision to homeschool need not be looked at as a long-range or unalterable choice. Indeed, many parents expect to keep their children at home only for the early years of schooling for a variety of reasons which will be covered in chapter 1.

Yes, you may choose to keep your children in school. But should they continue in public or private schools, you and your children will know how to make the most of other educational opportunities available to you. Anything homeschoolers do can be done after school or on the weekends to extend the education of your children. Though I must point out that homeschooling has as much to do with an attitude toward education as it does with any particular piece of information we teach our children or any specific activity we do with them.

Also important to note is that even if you do choose to keep your children enrolled in public or private school, you will now be making an informed choice. Your child may be thriving in school now, as many do, but that could change any time. You will know that you can always homeschool if school turns out to not work for your children.

As an aside, I think the term "homeschooling" is misleading. Homeschool parents aren't operating a school at home. Few of us stand at blackboards or use textbooks or give tedious assignments like, "Read the next chapter and answer the questions at the end." "Home-based education" would be a more accurate term, for home is the base we venture out from. We make use of all the amenities a home has to offer, like a fully stocked kitchen with ready snacks and meals, a TV with DVDs to be had on every interest imaginable, a low computer-to-person ratio, perhaps a garden or power tools in the garage, a car to take us anywhere we want to go on the spur of the moment, and much, much more. But we also spend a *lot* of time outside our homes interacting with other families and with the people in our community. We can easily take advantage of any interesting, educational, or just plain fun thing going on around us whether during school hours or not.

For over twenty years, I have been doing homeschool consulting to distressed parents of children who are having problems in school. The thing that brings me the most pleasure is hearing the relief in the parents' voices as they move from fear to confidence. It is my hope this book will do the same for you.

Exploring coastal geology to understand
how seismic activity shapes our world

Introduction

> *"It's a healthy thing, now and then, to hang a question mark on the things you have long taken for granted."*
> —Bertram Russell

A Quick Look at Your Own Experiences

If the information in this book is to be useful to you, it's important that you can see how it relates to your own experiences. Here is a short questionnaire to help start that process.

Write down on a blank sheet of paper or, better yet, in a notebook:

1. At least three things you are good at doing. These could be anything: reading, sewing clothes, balancing a checkbook, growing plants, crafts, getting along with people, driving safely, writing, home decorating, playing with children, hiking, sailing, fishing, drawing, algebra, etc.

2. At least three things that you love doing.

3. At least three things you are not good at doing.

4. At least three things you don't like to do.

5. Where or from whom you learned each thing.

Ponder Point

What conclusions can you draw from your answers?

How This Book Can Help You

Venturing into unknown waters can be intimidating. When parents feel they are doing so with their children's futures at risk, it can be downright terrifying. Most of today's parents are products of the U.S. public and private school systems, and few of us ever really thought there was any other way. Parents are even in a quandary about how much to help their children with their homework, much less what they could be doing to make sure their schooled child is actually getting a high quality and *relevant* education.

The Department of Education states on their web site that their budget for 2010 was $46.7 billion.[1] In 2010, a teacher's education could cost $6,585 per year at a four-year public college, $25,143 per year at private four-year college,[2] and over $40,000 at the top-five priciest U.S. universities.[3] To think we can do better ourselves sounds absolutely insane. Yet approximately one and a half million families in America homeschool,[4] and their children have, on average, outscored all other test takers on the ACT college entrance exams every year since 1997.[5] The cost of homeschooling can be virtually nothing for the family making judicious use of the public library, the Internet, and free community resources. A family buying the best packaged curricula, hiring tutors, and enrolling a child in private lessons could spend large amounts of money. An excellent education is possible in both cases and anything in between.

While the idea of homeschooling might seem radical to you, it's helpful to recognize that you're actually already teaching or "schooling" your children when they're not in school, both directly and by your role modeling. You can enrich their education at home using virtually everything you will read in this book.

If entirely homeschooling seems like too big a jump, it's probably for one of the following reasons:

1. Socialization

    - Will my children be social misfits?
    - Will they be friendless?

2. Academics

    - Will they learn what they're supposed to learn?
    - Will they be able to keep up?
    - Will they be able to go to college?

3. Instruction

    - Will I be able to motivate and teach them?
    - Will I have the patience?
    - What if I don't know the subject?
    - Where do I get materials?
    - Will I feel unfulfilled and bored being with my children all day?
    - Will I be able to afford to stay home to teach them?

These questions will all be addressed in this book.

I believe that for many (if not most) families, homeschooling is the best choice for raising and educating their children. Given the difficulties of modern life, including the world's economic and political uncertainties, homeschooling may offer you the best hope of preparing your children to be flexible adults who can think on their feet. Each week, month, and year spent in the embrace of the family helps strengthen a child to face an often capricious and challenging world. I encourage you to consider it. I hope this book proves useful in your decision making. At the very least, using the suggestions in this book will help you provide your children with more learning opportunities, enrich your family life, and strengthen the ties between your family members.

You'll also see that homeschooling is not an all-or-nothing proposition. Your children may end up being fully homeschooled, being fully schooled, or moving back and forth between the two. Furthermore, this book will give you a better idea on how to help your children get a quality education in any of these situations.

However, one caution I must give (and I wax a bit philosophical to say this) is that we can control our own behavior but we can't control the outcome. We can school or homeschool, parent well or badly, be strict or permissive, and yet we do not determine the futures of our children. We can only hope to turn the odds in our favor. You may do everything "right," and your child can have awful problems as an adult; conversely, you could do everything most would consider wrong, and yet, your child might become a happy, well-adjusted, successful adult. Nature, nurture, fate or God, and too many other variables make predicting the future with any certainty a difficult task.

What we do has more to do with ourselves and becoming and being the people we want to see in the mirror. We do this by seeking to be true to our highest values as we know them at this time and being open to changing when we see we fell short. We do our own homework, finding out what really works rather than just taking the easy way out and relying on our indoctrinated beliefs, on what our parents did, or just doing what is convenient at the time. We do our best to treat our children as we ourselves wish to be treated—we respect and listen to them and try to be the most kind, loving, understanding, fair parents we can be. We stumble, fail, get back up, and try again. If we do this, whatever the outcome for our children, we can sleep well at night knowing we did our best. Life is a journey, not a destination, as many have rightly said. May the journey you are taking with your children be the happiest, most fulfilling time of your lives.

The wonder of watching metamorphosis from
caterpillar to chrysalis to butterfly.

Chapter 1

Why Homeschool

Traditional Schooling: What, Why, and How Schools Teach

Most of us never question the hierarchical one-size-fits-most approach to education in our public and private schools. A government-mandated curriculum is followed by standardized tests in an attempt to ensure that children meet requirements. Children are all taught the same thing at the same age with the exception of gifted-and-talented and special-education children. Even the gifted-and-talented programs are often just accelerated versions of the government-issued curriculum. And special education can sometimes mean the student shows up, listens to his iPod the whole period, gets a D, and moves on to the next grade.

In fairness to the school system, consider the task of trying to set up a system to educate over fifty-three million highly diverse children.[6] They come from every type of family: from the severely impoverished or even homeless to the supremely wealthy, from those that speak little or no English to those that know multiple languages. Some children have never gone beyond their neighborhoods; others are world travelers. Some of their families are headed by a hardworking parent or parents, some by elderly grandparents or older siblings, some by folks struggling with poverty or mental illness, some by criminals. The children bring to the classroom the cultures of their races and areas of the country. Among them will be the artistic, the mechanical, the intellectual, and the athletic. Some will be bored, others troubled, mentally and emotionally challenged, or even drug addicted. Some are helpful; some are armed.

The system attempts to do what amounts to "herding cats" by adopting uniform standards for all students. Yet even these vary state to state. Given the diversity I just touched on, it's wonder anything gets done. And even in the best of circumstances, given the need to keep as many as thirty or more children busily occupied all day in a room, schools routinely run out of meaningful things to teach but still have to keep order. Thus, kids end up memorizing a list of state capitals and learning to divide negative fractions, and many other things that only a few of us remember or have ever found useful in our adult lives. All too often, the schools graduate students with good grades in all sorts of book knowledge and very little in the way of practical skills. For most students, college seems to have become a must to get a job doing almost anything. And college professors will tell you that much of their initial teaching is remedial.

If you take solace in the fact that your child is enrolled

in a private school, you may have a false sense of security. Often, students who cause trouble in public schools are sent to private schools in hopes they'll be straightened out. These kids tend to need extra teacher attention or may continue to be disruptive, again distracting serious students from their studies.

Let's have a look at what John Taylor Gatto, schoolteacher for thirty years, former New York teacher of the year, and world-renowned author and public speaker, had to say about our school system:

"My kids don't know what a mile is, not really, although I think they could pass a test on it. In similar fashion, they don't know what democracy is, or what money is, or what an economy is, or how to fix anything. They've heard of Mogadishu and Saddam Hussein, but they couldn't tell you the name of the tree outside their window if their life depended on it... Some of them can do quadratic equations, but they can't sew a button on a shirt or fry an egg; they can bubble in answers with a number two pencil, but they can't build a wall. Many of them have no idea that most of the men and women on earth believe in God, or how that might affect the way they live.

"... The truth is that my kids are unable to plot a future because they don't know where they are or who they are. How can you know who you are if you don't know your own family, and how can you know your own family if none of you are home together very often? Who arranged things this way, because surely they didn't just happen."[7]

Many of us have ideas about how schools might be changed, but that is beyond the scope of this book. Education is a gigantic, entrenched, powerful bureaucracy, and the many serious attempts to improve it have met with massive resistance. Most of what is called "reform" amounts to no more than tinkering around the edges. The constant testing required by the No Child Left Behind Act leaves little time for imaginative teachers hoping to inspire their students.

> *"The things that matter most should never be at the mercy of the things that matter least."*
> —Johann Wolfgang von Goethe

However it may seem, none of this is meant as school bashing. I honestly believe that school administrators and teachers mean well and that most are truly idealistic and altruistic. And some schools still manage to do a decent job of educating many of their students. But is school the best place for your children to spend the bulk of their youth?

Are their school peers a good influence? Or are your children learning behaviors at odds with your values? Are they getting physical activity and the enrichment of the arts? Or have these activities been pushed aside by a total focus on academics? Are they socializing with people of differing ages, cultures, and ethnic groups? Or is their socialization limited to the confines of a clique? Are they learning from real books and real people who have experienced the real world? Are they learning the actual skills of living? Or are they doing rote learning, memorizing, and then forgetting bits of facts rehashed in mind-numbing textbooks? Are their unique qualities being respected and developed? Or are they being trained into a mold?

> *"To be nobody but yourself in a world which is doing its best day and night to make you like everybody else, means to fight the hardest battle which any human being can fight and never stop fighting."*
>
> —e.e. cummings

Socialization

One of the first things most people ask when the subject of homeschooling comes up is, "What about socialization?" This question seems to come from the rather strange idea that children teach other children social skills. Where did such an idea come from? Certainly for the bulk of human history, children were socialized by their families. They spent their waking hours intimately interacting with their parents and siblings, their grandparents, aunts, uncles, cousins, friends, neighbors, church members, and business people. Adults taught, corrected, and modeled how to behave in a wide range of social situations with people of different ages, genders, church and party affiliations, skills, and professions. Children even learned from farm animals and their social patterns. They saw births and deaths.

Children ate, slept, read, and did real work with their family and community and experienced the importance of working together. An adult was generally nearby to answer questions or show them how to do something, be it bake a pie, help with the harvest, sew a garment, or read. These are the children who have a sense of self-worth based on real-life demonstrations of competence and know when their needs must take the backseat to real-life problems.

Now we've been led to believe that children must be taken out of that diverse environment and isolated from society in a room with thirty peers and one or two teachers in order to learn good behavior. Those of us who have spent any time at all in a classroom will tell you otherwise.

Parents and children help each other identify
birds by sight, flight pattern and behavior.

Parents sometimes feel that child is supposed to have (fewer, more, different) friends and that a school setting will solve that. Friendship is a tricky thing to judge for someone else. Sometimes, a child with one best friend learns more about friendship than a child with lots of associations. Some children thrive on variety. Some shy children prefer a rowdy friend and vice versa. In any case, with home as a base, parent can more easily respond to the ever-changing social needs of their children.

You may be surprised to hear that fellow parents and I can often tell how long a child has been in school before joining our homeschool community. We can see this by the amount of *antisocial* behavior he or she displays—bullying, teasing, premature sexuality, profanity, drug and alcohol use, cliquishness, and prejudice against others because of their gender, race, skin color, clothes, height, weight, or glasses. It seems children will use any difference as an excuse to exclude and torment. We all know of the catastrophic results of these behaviors in far too many tragedies.

Fortunately, we have also found that the positive environment within our group soon calms down the bad behavior formerly schooled children bring to it. My guess is that this is how it happens in homeschool groups elsewhere as well.

Dr. Raymond Moore, former teacher, principal, and superintendent of California public schools wrote about his extensive research on this topic.

"We later became convinced that little children are not only better taught at home than at school, but also better socialized by parental example and sharing than by other little children...Contrary to common beliefs, little children are not best socialized by other kids; the more persons around them, the fewer meaningful contacts...Negative, me-first sociability is born from more peer group association and fewer meaningful parental contacts and responsibility experiences in the home during the first eight to twelve years. The early peer influence generally brings an indifference to family values which defy parents' correction.[8]

If you want to give your children a good foundation of healthy social skills and peer-pressure proof them, teach them yourself for as long as you are able, at least during those critical early years.

Academics

Besides the importance of teaching valuable, positive social skills in the first ten to twelve years, there are also very good reasons to wait to present academic materials to your children.

Child development experts have long observed that children are not physically or mentally ready for formal education much before they are eight or ten. Jean Piaget (1896–1980) [9] was one of the early researchers on this subject and found there were definite stages appropriate for the success of various kinds of learning. Pushing children into learning for which they weren't ready was asking for failure or behavior problems. Abstract thinking, he found, begins around age twelve.

Parents often note the enthusiasm among youngsters for the first few grades and the pride the children show in naming numbers and letters. They almost uniformly say they love school. Even third graders, when I asked them how they liked school, would answer in the affirmative. But by middle school, few children told me they loved school, and this is the time when I am most likely to receive a call from the desperate parents of suffering school children. When we see the school-related problems increasing through the years, we surely must question the push for early academics and the burnout it produces.

A mismatch between developmental levels and school requirements is one source of the problem here, especially for boys. They will most likely be labeled as behavior problems and diagnosed with some version of attention deficit and hyperactivity. Girls also have attention problems too but are less likely to be diagnosed, because they are not as easily recognized[10]. These children aren't ready to sit still at a desk for long periods of time, unable to talk, or move around at will. The solution to this issue in school is likely to be bribery (rewards), discipline (punishment), drugs, or separation into classes with other children who have problems in the regular classroom.

Most in the homeschool community have experienced or heard stories of other families who have experienced problems which vanished once the child was no longer attending school. Lanet Abrigo's piece (see Chapter 1, Parents in Their Own Words) is one such story.

Alternative schools, such as Montessori and Waldorf, do a reasonable job teaching children age-appropriate knowledge and motor skills—though they often have to resist the pressure from parents to begin early academics. These schools also endeavor to impart social skills and healthy values, working to develop the character of the students. The successes they have are due in part to their very small class size, which makes them more closely resemble a family than a school. Still, even their programs may not be a good fit for your children at any given time, and teachers will have to work at techniques to motivate them to do what is expected and prevent them from doing the things they prefer.

At home, we can tailor the studies to the child, eliminating the need for bribes and punishments. We can teach that learning is worthwhile for its own sake, that knowledge is a pleasure to have, and that we especially enjoy learning about the things we are interested in. Children can learn how to do things that matter to them. We can instill a lifelong love of learning by being attuned to their passions and needs at the time.

Engrossed in a book of his own choosing,
he continues to be an avid reader as an adult.

We also must question how much children parrot what they hear from their parents about how much they will love school and how school is necessary to succeed. Our own son was told by third graders that he would never get a job if he didn't go to school. Third graders concerned with getting a job? Where has childhood gone?

I would always tell Thumper that it probably was true—he would likely never "get a job" if he didn't go to school. But what he would have was a career, a calling, and he has turned out to be quite the entrepreneur. He had a temporary job recently where he helped prepare the facilities at Camp Woodward before camp started. He came away from that experience with a real appreciation for how hard people with jobs work and how little they get paid. He was even more thankful that he didn't have to work at a nine-to-five job but instead had created a lucrative career for himself as a freelance videographer.

As for academics in the intermediate and high school years, learning the subjects in a standard curriculum goes much faster and easier at home without the distractions of unruly classmates. Older children will have ample time to cover those and still have time left over to delve more deeply into the subjects and activities they are passionate about. They are often ready for early college entrance.

I Never Set Out to Be a Homeschooler!

I am a product of the public school system, as I am sure you, the reader, are. I had never really considered that there might be another way to get an education. I got good grades at a time when that meant something and graduated from a top-tier university with honors.

After graduation, I was faced with the real world and was responsible for big life choices. For seventeen years in the school system, my path had been clear—read the next chapter, answer the questions at the end, write the term paper, do the next course, start the next semester. Now I found myself wondering what that was all for and feeling that somehow I had missed some important lessons. But I still didn't question standard educational theory. It was many years later that I realized that not much of my schooling was of practical use in my daily life nor was it helpful in leading a meaningful life.

I spent the next twenty years teaching, giving and receiving personal counseling, writing, painting watercolors, and learning about nutrition and fitness, politics and nature, and all sorts of other things I found interesting and useful. I met and married my husband, and we decided it was time to have a baby.

About that time, we heard of a course at the Institutes for the Achievement of Human Potential[11] in Philadelphia called "How to Multiply Your Baby's Intelligence."[12] Everything about the Institutes sounded impressive, so we flew out for the one-week class at their elegant facility. I'm not sure we thought this thing through, but somehow it made sense that we could make our child physically, emotionally, and intellectually advantaged through intense teaching starting at birth. He would skip grades, go off to an Ivy League college in his early teens, and have a hugely successful career in some admired field of endeavor like medicine or law. We left Philadelphia armed with ideas, materials, and high expectations.

As soon as our son, Thumper, was born, I jumped in with the program. For the first six or eight months, it went well. Using flashcards, I'd taught him to recognize everything from vocabulary words to insects and presidents. The program's activities led to his hearing, sight, and motor skills being somewhat advanced for his age. Then he started letting me know that despite my enthusiastic presentations, he was no longer amused by the word-and-picture knowledge I had been taught was worthwhile. It may have been helpful for some children, but it was not for our son.

I had the first glimmer of doubt about the program, and I began dropping parts of the academic activities. Eventually I came to realize that if I was simply open to Thumper, I could easily discover his needs at any given time. He became my best teacher.

With a bit of childproofing, he was free to explore his world and make sense of it without interference or having to be coerced into it. He loved the water, so we went to the beach nearly every day. He wanted to explore the yard, the house, stores, the TV, the kitchen, paints, dirt, tools—*everything* was now a fascinating learning experience.

We had always explored these things, but now we did so without worry or apology for what we *should* be doing. We were all having fun learning new things, and we became even closer as a family.

When Thumper turned three, the other children we knew went off to preschool, and their caretakers went back to work. It still didn't make sense to send him away, so I started a playgroup so we would have children and adults to play with. Many of these people became our lifelong friends.

While children going to preschool were better at letters or counting and such, certainly none were more curious, more eager to learn, more full of life, and more fun to be with than our son. And I doubt there were happier parents anywhere.

But what about when it was time for school? In my seventeen years of schooling, I had learned the factory model of education with its top-down curriculum, and this had been seconded by the class in Philadelphia. It was what I'd been prepared to perpetuate. But by now I had begun to suspect that it was presumptuous to think any school or government bureaucrat—or even I—could know best what bits of knowledge would serve him in twenty or more years hence in a world changing with dizzying speed. I knew I had to give this some serious thought.

I approached the subject with the beginner's mind described by Zen Master Shunryu Suzuki: "The mind of the beginner is empty, free of the habits of the expert, ready to accept, to doubt, and open to all the possibilities. It is the kind of mind which can see things as they are, which step by step and in a flash can realize the original nature of everything."[13]

To educate myself on our choices during those years, I devoured piles of books and magazines. More importantly, I observed our son, other children, and other families. I scrutinized my beliefs and upbringing, and I questioned the doctrines I had been surrounded with in my own childhood and schooling.

Child development researchers recommended delaying school until age eight or nine, when a child's mind and body are more ready to address academic materials.[14] That made sense to me, especially when I looked at my boisterous, energetic son. It was obvious that he would be stifled by the desk-and-pencil learning typical in schools.

We knew that schools, such as Waldorf and Montessori, are based on these discoveries about childhood developmental stages and needs. While these schools work well for many children, when we got a Waldorf curriculum for kindergarten, we found ourselves departing from it more often than following it. Even these progressive programs can have a dogma which may not fit with a particular child's needs at any given time.

Over the years, we became more and more trusting of the process of curiosity-driven education, often termed "unschooling." I actually prefer the phrase "learning without schooling," as it expresses the notion that learning takes place all the time, not just in the confines of school. Indeed, more learning happens in less time without schooling, because the learner is self-motivated and not distracted by the antics of other children bucking the system or by the busywork that the system uses to keep children occupied so many hours each day.

Delaying school for Thumper meant we again needed more peers to relate to, since most kids were now in school and their parents both worked. I started a homeschool support group: HAPPY (Homeschool Adventures: Program for Parents and Youngsters).

Working with wire of various gage and color to create sculpture pieces.

I scheduled weekly activities ranging from doing crafts, going on camping trips and whale watch cruises to field trips to the crash rescue fire department at the airport, a dry cleaner, a ballet studio, a solar observatory atop Haleakala Volcano, and uncountable other interesting places. We sometimes had more than fifty people participating in an activity. We did community service projects ranging from picking up trash to caroling to elderly shut-ins and making crafts for the women's shelter and our servicemen. Our home was referred to as "Hotel Nagasako," because we always seemed to have children, both homeschooled and traditionally schooled, staying with us.

I tried a few workbooks in those first years, and they had their place for when I was busy. But they were such a contrived way to learn and only held Thumper's interest for short periods of time in the early years. We found that our life naturally led into relevant learning experiences. We explored our world, read stacks of books about things we were interested in, and met scores of interesting people of all ages. My husband, meanwhile, had started a business and was working hard to provide our family with the necessities and to enable me to stay home with our son.

Thumper's eighth and ninth birthdays had come and gone, and we were still not ready to commit him to spending his day limited to a classroom with thirty kids exactly his age and one or two adults. We had the whole world in which to play and learn. And by this time we had had ample chances to observe how schooled kids behaved. We wanted none of that.

As a family, we just kept putting one foot in front of the other, working together to create lives we found rich and rewarding. We learned U.S. geography from airplane windows on our travels to visit family and to go to most of his competitions. As of this writing, Thumper's business and athletic competitions have taken him to fifteen states, the District of Columbia and to Canada, England, Germany, Italy, Russia, and France. While he had seen pictures of the Vatican, the Sistine Chapel, and the Berlin Wall before, he's also been there in person. In fact, it was he who led us around the Louvre, finding the most famous works of art.

Now I don't want to leave the impression that one

needs to travel afar to learn. I have been stunned to see how many schooled children know so little about their own communities, local politics and economics, plants, the food they eat, the weather, and the sky above them.

We've watched meteor showers and taken adult astronomy classes. We've dug for Indian fossils in Michigan and antique bottles here in Hawaii. We've learned about the world around us and our own geography and history. Thumper learned his writing skills not by drills and school essays, but by writing many letters to his grandparents, résumés for his sponsors, and scripts for his videos and web sites. All along, he pursued his passion, in-line skating, and taught himself complex computer and video skills, so he could make videos of himself and others practicing the sport.

He did take a day tour of an intermediate school when he was thirteen just to see if he wanted to go to school. He came away from that experience knowing he wanted to continue to homeschool. His description of his day and how he felt about it is in the next section of this chapter.

We were probably as surprised as anyone when he turned sixteen and still had not gone to school. At that time, we set up another tour, this time of the local high school, and he decided to give it a try and enrolled as a junior. He went for three semesters, getting all As, except for one B, before he left out of sheer boredom and frustration over spending so many hours there and getting so little done. He went on to get his GED, which uses graduating high school seniors as the control group so the GED score can serve as a ranking among his schooled peers nationally.[15] He scored in the top 13 percent overall and in the top 1 percent for literature. He has taken classes at the local community college and the University of Hawaii, getting a similar GPA to his high school results.

Thumper is now twenty-eight and has put his video and editing skills into a fulfilling career as an event videographer. He is also a professional vert[16] in-line skater, having won the ASA World Amateur Championship in 2002. He finished his rookie year as the number-one-ranked American, fourth in the world. He's been ranked in the top ten worldwide each year since, including at the X Games and Gravity Games.

Thumper tests a new camera.
http://www.hifocused.com[17]

Would I do it differently if I'd known then what I know now? Sure, there are bits and pieces I might do differently—like perhaps working part time when he was older so I didn't suffer so much when he flew the nest. But overall, I am grateful that we were able to homeschool for so long. We learned so much together and had so much fun doing it. We have many great memories; I was present for all of his "firsts." I appreciate the close ties we have now as a family and his confident independence. I am grateful for all those years of not having to worry about him being "left behind" or whether he was safe or whether he was being influenced unduly by peer pressure. We had no teen rebellion; what would he rebel against? We always respected him and worked with him, helping him achieve his goals. I am grateful for the grace that led me to trust in him and in the intrinsic desire of all living things to grow, learn, and improve.

Children and Young Adults in Their Own Words

I asked these individuals for their views of homeschooling. None of them had any idea what the others were writing. You will note certain themes run through all of the testimonials, while the particulars of how and what they studied differ. Some went to school a few years, some for many years, some not at all. Some have gone on to college; one is a graduate with multiple degrees. One is a schooled child I know who wrote her story to me without prompting.

From Nani Jenson, a former homeschooler
now enrolled in a San Diego college:

As I sit at my high school graduation ceremony and look around at my proud class, I realize that all of us are so delighted to be graduating—not because we are finally going to prove our worth in the world, but rather that we are free from the chains of school. In an institution where they congratulate clones rather than free thinking, I wonder how I made it through all four years.

I was homeschooled up until fourth grade, and in that time I actually got to experience what being a child really means, listening to my body tell me when I was hungry or needed to use the restroom, not a bell or authority figure. I got to explore things others just watched in "informative" videos, and, most importantly, I got to be free and begin my active role into becoming who I am today.

School has taught me many things about life, but mainly it was what I learned from observing others and the function of the institution, not from the actual teachings themselves. I learned how to procrastinate and miss a horrendous number of days and still obtain a 4.2 grade point average. I learned how to stand up for myself against my superiors without crossing the line. But mainly, I learned that those who never truly got to experience a childhood were the most childish in my classes.

Wendy plays with Nani as a baby.
Wendy homeschooled all the way through
high school and is now married and a mother
herself. Nani is a junior in college in San Diego

Life is meant to be lived and although I do not regret my decision for entering school, I will always be thankful to my parents for giving me the childhood that is so absent for kids schooled from the earliest ages.

From a child who wishes she could be homeschooled and who gets all As at a private school:

We have art class every Tuesday for an hour. Today we were studying Georgia O'Keeffe. And we took a fake flower—we do this *every* year—and we used pastels to draw it. Today wasn't very fun because I thought I was done, because I colored it all in and I really liked it. So I went up to show my art teacher my picture. Then she told me I was going too fast and I needed to slow down. But what's the point of going slow when you can go fast, like I do, and still have it be very, *very* good? And she made me change *a lot!* By the time she said *she* liked it, I *hated it!* She does that so much! I think we should have an art teacher who lets us stop when we think it's the best we can do and when we like it. It's really frustrating.

From Lili Story, age seventeen, who writes about "What homeschooling means to me."

Homeschooling gives me the freedom and opportunity to be an individual. At home I can pursue those interests and ways of being that make me unique. I have been able to remain very close with my family, too, and this is really important to me.

Because my days are flexible, I created my own summer businesses and incorporated them into my learning. I have gained hands-on experience in a number of real-life skills that I most likely wouldn't have had otherwise.

One of the most special things in my life is my participation in a wonderful outdoor youth program, through which I have grown tremendously. I am in my third year with this program and it has changed my life. It also encompasses much of what I love to do, like hiking, studying plants, and seeing wild animals. Other things I love include playing the piano, growing food, drawing, knitting, roller-skating, dancing, cooking, and lots more!

And last but not least, because I homeschool I have retained my love of learning and natural curiosity, which I believe is very instrumental in creating any kind of success and enjoying life to its fullest.

From Lili's sister, Rio Story, age nine:

Being homeschooled has really changed what my life could have been. I still do school work, of course, but I have so much fun. This week I put on my tool belt and got up on the roof of the house we are building. I have done so many other things like pouring concrete, cutting rebar, cantering horses, and playing and working on our farm.

So life as a homeschooler is great.

Introduction to Thumper's story

When Thumper was thirteen, he went on a field trip *to* school, his first time *ever* inside school walls. He has been unschooled all his life. About a year before, my husband and I started to feel it was time for him to see for himself what school was like. We had several reasons for this: Thumper was concerned about how his knowledge compared to that of his friends in school, kids were always telling him how much fun it was to be with friends all day, and it seemed to me that a well-rounded education would include personal experience of the institution where most others spend their youth. I have always been an advocate of the joys and advantages of homeschooling, and we felt that only by experiencing school for himself could Thumper decide whether homeschooling or going to school would be best for him. He agreed so we arranged for him to attend school—eighth grade—all day with a friend.

As preparation, we discussed with Thumper various situations that might come up and how he might handle them. We had his friend over and asked him to describe his exact schedule of classes. We wanted to know what work was being done in each class and what to expect at recess and lunch. The following week, we did what we could to prepare him for the classes.

When the day arrived, we were both extremely nervous, and when I drove away from the school that morning, my stomach was churning.

From Thumper, after his first day of school at age thirteen.[18]

...Lots of kids bring candy to school—no wonder they don't do well in school. Math class seemed real easy. So far, everything they've done, I knew. We flicked these spinners to figure batting averages and I'm thinking, *We're just flicking spinners and writing down on the little chart!* By then I was overwhelmed with boredom....One kid was teasing this one girl in class that they play baseball with, and I didn't really like that, but I guess that's just how it is.

Then we went over to recess and got some grub. The food looked like some sort of chunks of meat, but it had all different kinds of bones in it going all different directions. I ate a little—I had to get the feeling of eating cafeteria food—and it gave me a little stomachache, but I was okay.

We saw this little scuffle at recess. One guy is going toward this other guy, and a huge guy is holding him back. My friend had told me that these guys could pick fights, so I was worried about that. But they're in their own little gang thing, and they're worried about gang guys against them, not just regular guys walking around.

Next we went into the weight lifting class, and all they did in that class was talk about muscles and tendons. All the kids were just talking to [the teacher], talking about fighting, and the teacher's saying, "I don't mess with anybody that can beat me up, but if I think I can beat them up..." I forgot what he said, but out of all the teachers, he seemed the most macho.

General sports, math, and computer—those didn't even actually seem like actual classes with tables or anything lined up or in groups. They could put their chairs where they wanted and one kid even sat at the teacher's desk.

Then business. You haven't been in hell if you haven't been in business. When we went in, Jack says, "Yeah! The cruise class." And like every class I saw him at, he waits until a couple of minutes after the bell rings and then goes into the class and the teacher's just setting things up or unlocking the door. Not very professional.

When I went in, I gave the teacher the note and she says, "I'll introduce you." She's going, "Class! Class! Hey, you, sit down! Charlie, come on man, sit down! And you, stop walking around! Come on, sit down! Everybody sit down! Stop playing with those things!" Then she turns to me and says, "Sorry. It's like this every day!"

Some kids dragged four desks in the back and put the fan behind me and the rubbish can next to me and tried to move the bookshelf and recycling bins over there and they were all just goofing off and rearranging the class. Then the teacher scolded them, and they put everything back.

Lenny draws a face on his finger and he puts it through a hole in this little part of the fan and he's going, "Hi kids! Look at me—I'm Skippy the sandworm. Everybody, say hi to Skippy the sandworm." And another kid's hiding behind the rubbish can and they're running around acting as if they're holding guns and [the teacher]'s going, "Sit down you guys, get the show on." She's just yelling at them and when she saw the kids opening and closing the vents, she said, "Fine, if you want it to get hot in here, it's your problem." And she's yelling at them, and the kids are on the side opening and closing vents and then this kid turns out the light and starts to close the door. It started to go almost black in the room, and she got everything together and then got the lights turned on. Guys are talking in class while she's explaining. And I asked Jack, "What kind of grades do you get?" expecting, "Oh, D or D+ or something," but he goes, "Oh, Bs—this class is so cruise."

The teacher had this piece of paper for kids to copy what it says and Jack walks up, tears it down, and grabs the one underneath and puts the first one back up, and it just falls on the floor and the kids are supposed to be copying it. And he tries to put it back up, but it just falls down, and he walks away and makes the other one into a sort of cone and he says, "Look at me, I'm the flying nun," and he runs around the class flapping his arms and going, "Do do do." He sits back down with the paper and copies it and then he gave it back later. Then he walked over and grabs a hall pass and walks out of the room.

But man, they were goofing off so much there. Then [the teacher]'s in the middle of explaining something and Lenny says, "It's army time," and he crumples up this piece of paper into a long piece and holds it up and says, "This is my telescope." He should have said "periscope." And he holds it up and makes like he's looking through it, and then he jumps up in the middle of the aisle and lays down on his stomach and crawls with his arms looking through his periscope and a couple of guys follow and they're acting like they're wielding guns, and one guy is crawling around on his knees around the aisle, and the whole forty-five minutes, she only got about five sentences said.

I asked Jack, "If you could have any class all day, what would it be?"

He answered, "This one."

I asked, "Why?" and he says, "It's so cruise." And I think, *Man, he would rather not learn anything at all and just kick back than learn. Just waste time.* It was fun and all, but after a while, it's got to be total boredom to the other kids and a waste of time. He'd rather spend his time in a cruise class wasting his time than in classes not goofing off and learning a bunch of stuff he could apply!

Man, I've never seen chaos till I've been in there! Another kid skips around the room with the cone on his head while [the teacher]'s not looking. And when she's talking to the some other kids, they turn their backs to her. At the end of the class they got a talking-to and she's all going, "What's wrong with you guys? What're you guys doing?"

They told me, "Every week they say that to us, but we'd

be good the next day...[T]hen the next week we'll be bad again and she just won't do anything." You should've seen how many threats she made to them.

"You'll get detention all spring break. I'll call your parents. We'll get you kicked out of the school." But it never happens. Every day it's like that.

Then there was lunch. We're sitting on the curb just doing nothing. And a kid says, "Oh look, there's Frank, let's go tease him." and the other kids say, "Yeah! All right! Let's go!" and they all go. He's throwing rubbish into the rubbish bin and Lenny takes one piece of it back out and throws it in the bushes and Jack says, "Eh, heh! You dropped it. Eh, heh, ey, you wuss!" teasing him and [Frank] says, "F--- you," and he's looking like he's going to cry and the guy's putting him down. If this was happening in my territory, like at the skate park, I'd say, "Leave him alone," but since it's in someone else's territory, I thought, *Just don't do anything, just watch, just observe, I'm observing*. Then [Frank] went away carrying the rubbish cans and he was all mad and stuff. I felt sorry for him.

Next was English. This was actually the realest class we were in. We sat down and she says to write a five-paragraph essay and back it up with facts. While they wrote, I wrote:

"What I've observed so far:

"To me, school seems a lot more slacked off than I thought it would be like. The work seems pretty easy... The activities seem pretty stupid and maybe a little too easy for them. Seems like I could catch on real fast. I know most of the stuff already, I think. The teachers seem pretty unprofessional. They let lots of kids talk and seem to just ask, then yell, then threaten."

Anyway, then we went into social studies and that class... seemed pretty easy.

And then we rode the bus, and [there] was loud, pounding music, guys just all talking, and the bus driver's yelling at the kids. And I was thinking, *Man, I don't know how this school thing can work for the kids, for the teachers, the bus drivers, the so-called cooks. I don't know how they do it—I don't know how they even survive! They must somehow adapt some sort of blankness in their brains, which makes them be totally resistant to boredom.*

It took me until last night to realize it's over! I've been to school. I've seen the demon in its eyes, and I can't believe it! It's like I was in a daze, and I actually realized I've been to school and I've seen what everybody thought the big deal is and it's just totally boring! They think what they're doing is so great—they should be in my life. I guess for some kids, it's like nicotine—you know you hate it, you know it's unhealthy and not good for you, but it's addictive. You get a craving for it or something.

I feel I could do well in school. And I feel that the work I do at home is just as hard as or harder than the work they're doing in school. Like I could probably get the school day's work done in forty-five minutes and the stuff I usually do takes me about two hours. It's amazing how slow it goes! They say you got to learn, and I should say, "Yeah, you really do."

Three weeks later:

"I just can't believe it's over. It's been a year since I thought of checking out school. And now that I have, I'm just so stoked how it turned out! I'm so glad I'm homeschooling! I used to feel dumb when I would mess up, but to see how much I get done compared to them, I feel real good about my education [and] my intelligence, and life overall is great!

I also heard it was this big social scene and it wasn't. There was about as much taunting and hassling as I expected, and it seemed like the kids were just school friends. It didn't seem too social to me.

The school experience made me a lot more extroverted, and it put everything in perspective. Now I don't get so embarrassed if I say something stupid, and I'm more willing to goof off and crack jokes in front of more people. I feel more confident in myself and that I'm doing the right thing with my life.

From Paz Padilla, one of five homeschooled children in his family:

Homeschooling for me was an exploration of myself and of the world around me. It allowed me to develop my uniqueness as an individual. I was able to grow in any and all directions, and like a plant freed from its pot, I flourished. I was given the tools to learn and was free to learn whatever I wanted. That in turn taught me the importance of responsibility as well as the value of the moment. I will be forever grateful for the opportunity to have been homeschooled.

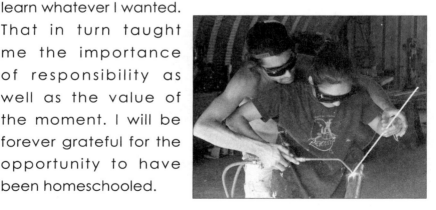

Paz teaches his younger sister, Gina, how to braze brass to copper.

29

From Georgia Amber Pinsky, a recent college graduate:

My educational background is somewhat of a novelty. Homeschooled K-12, I can say that I never set foot in school until I went to earn my GED. Although I had very little structured schooling, I needed only twelve hours of classes to prepare for and pass the test. A few months later, I enrolled in classes at Maui Community College. I was seventeen.

To start at the beginning, when I was three, my brother came to join our family. When I was five, my parents enrolled me in the nearby Waldorf school, but come the first day of school, they "couldn't bear to part with my company," or so my dad told me years later. (I think they liked the idea of an in-house babysitter.)

But seriously, my brother and I grew up together, learning the intricacies of sibling relationships and caring for our many, many animals—dogs, cats, horses, chickens, and ducks, and for a time, two bull calves. I had the responsibility to feed, water, keep dry, love, and nurture numerous creatures before I was ten. In retrospect, I can see that the responsibility granted to my brother and me has greatly influenced who we are. While my friends spent their days doing...umm, the multiplication tables or something, I was repairing the chicken coop, or exercising the horses, or building a tree house. My dad trusted me fully since the beginning, or so it feels. My mom has taken a little longer. My parents gave me chances to mess up, in real ways, and also to have real victories. Grades, SATs, and cliques do not real character build.

Without the stress of trying to be accepted, I was able to stretch and become who I am meant to be. As this me was forming, it was not challenged or limited, but more often encouraged and supported. I've come to put it this way,

"Each of us, our character, for purposes of this analogy, takes a square shape. The act of trying to be accepted by peers, earning good grades consistently, etc., is a circle hoop to jump through. As you jump through the hoop, it shaves off the corners of your character so you can fit through the hoop."

Today I am twenty-six, and I recently completed a nine-year experience in the University of Hawaii system. That sounds like a lot to my peers, but I remind them that I completed nine years of institutional schooling total, not on top of an original twelve. When I first enrolled at Maui Community College, I was not there with [the] intention of completing a degree. After five years there, I had exhausted the course catalog with As and Bs and transferred to UH Hilo to complete my degree in technical performing arts. Two years later, and four or five classes short of completing that degree, I switched my major to communication. I now hold a BA in communication.

I strongly encourage all parents to take the time and effort to educate themselves on the way to best nurture their children. In closing, I know that I am the beautiful person I am today because I was allowed to skip the system until I was ready to embrace it.

Parents in Their Own Words

From Mary Jo Padilla who, along with her husband, Larry, homeschooled five children and developed a very successful family business:

I first met Gail in 1987 when I was trying to decide whether to homeschool my two boys who were in kindergarten and second grade at the time. I was a bit nervous about being teacher as well as mom. After meeting Gail and her son,

Thumper, and getting involved with her homeschool group, we decided to homeschool and continued to do so with all five of our children. She helped me to see that education could be a natural part of life, and we shared many days together with our children having fun and learning at the same time.

Each of our children had a different path of education from the others:

Kaleo was homeschooled for third and fourth grade, and then went to a Waldorf school and from there to the elite college preparatory high school, Seabury Hall. He graduated from Claremont McKenna College with a bachelor's degree in economics and is now chief of operations for Padilla Designs.

Janus homeschooled twelve years, most of it at home, some at Hui Malama Learning Center. He earned his GED, scoring in the top 5 percent of the nation, and attended Maui Community College for two years, starting at sixteen. He did fine there both academically and socially, and is now an engineer and designer for Padilla Designs, as are his two younger brothers.

Paz, Thumper, Janus, and Kaleo have
a great time on a canoe.

Paz homeschooled and attended Hui Malama until high school and then attended a private school, playing tennis there all four years until graduation.

Ian homeschooled until high school and then attended and graduated from public school.

Gina went to elementary school intermittently, mostly homeschooling until eighth grade. She attended a private school for two years and then went to public school, graduating with honors. She went to [the] University of Hawaii for a year and attended Maui Community College for a year and is now working part time in the family business.

Our homeschooling was life-based, with our children participating in every kind of sports, reading voraciously, and taking classes, such as pottery, tap dancing, and gymnastics. We raised chickens, ducks, goats, peacocks, and turkeys, and we gardened. Through our early family life, we had challenges in our living situation. At one time we lived a very frugal life financially, but rich all other ways. Our home was a very old, tiny, dilapidated place we called the Banyan Tree House after the tree that spread over it more than a fourth of an acre. Life there was carefree, with days spent at the beach, reading, taking family outings, and developing our now very successful family business.

Because their dad, Larry, and I have always worked at home, we have had, and continue to have, a very close family. Larry taught them all sorts of skills, including how to weld at age six. We always had a houseful of other children, both schooled and homeschooled, so we had abundant social contact with the kids and their families. All the boys are avid outdoorsmen, and if I had to be dropped into the wilderness, I would want them at my side.

Larry and I are so grateful for the children we've been blessed with and the life we have created together.

From the mother of a schooled child, who
relays what her daughter told her:

I [am] once again frustrated with what Jessica is going through. She had science homework yesterday that involved mass, volume, [and] density stuff, and the book mentioned little experiments you can do to measure things (like putting a rock in a measuring cup of water to determine its volume). Anyway, she said they never do those in class, just read the chapters and supposedly learn it that way. How awful is that! She did say once in a while they meet with the sixth graders to do experiments that they make up themselves, but I'm not sure how that's working out—it sounds like they just end up goofing around.

Of course, I got out a measuring cup, and we tried different things and had some fun. Tomorrow is parent-teacher conference, so maybe I'll ask if I can come in once in a while to do a science lab. Science is such a hands-on subject; I couldn't believe they're just "book learning."

Jessica says when they are doing worksheets in class (yeah, I know, another useless way to learn), the teacher gets tired of waiting for them to finish (or maybe it's just time to move on to the next mandated subject) and just gives them the answers. My son, Robert, would like that, but Jessica sees it as unfair because she would know the answers without being told, but can't show it if the teacher gives everybody the answers anyway.

From Melisa Schwarm, *mother of now fourteen-year-old Otto, seen in many of the photos in this book.*

(She wrote their story when he was six and reports they have stayed true to the same course in their approach to his education. She and her husband Doug are delighted with the young man they see emerging from the boy they have been homeschooling all along.)

Let me start with what our educational goals are for Otto:

1. We always want him to approach the life process of learning with enthusiasm.

2. We want him to be driven by his own goals.

3. We want him to derive self-esteem from pride in how he conducts himself while striving toward his goals, rather than needing praise for what he has accomplished.

To this end we have decided to free school. Some people call it unschooling, but in any case, it means learning without following a preset curriculum. We decided not to follow somebody else's schedule of the timing, age, grade, or sequence in which Otto should learn. He, like other young children, is a sponge. He just absorbs information without it being presented to him in a "now it is time to learn this" fashion. We believe in teachable moments—those times when he is trying to get a grasp on an idea but he needs a little clarification in order for it to make sense to him in a meaningful way. We stop whatever else we are doing and use the advantage of his curiosity to help him with this learning experience so that the new information learned will be integrated into his greater understanding of the world.

So what does this mean practically, on a day-to-day basis? It means he spends a lot of his time in unstructured, non-directed play. It means he has a lot of freedom and a lot of personal responsibility. His decisions and actions have consequences and we see him learning cause and effect from his experiences. It means we minimize the struggle as we walk through the few "must-do's" of our day, like getting gas for the car or grocery shopping. It means we might have a reading lesson at 10:00 p.m. or a geometry lesson in the car if that is the time when his young mind is ready for our help to clarify what he is struggling to learn. We see that the things he has learned this way are permanently integrated into his knowledge of the world, and that he retains what he has come to understand because the learning has meaning for him.

When I speak of our philosophy to those who ask, I am often met with objections to our approach because people think he will not want to learn some essential knowledge that we all must have in order to be fully functional, successful adults in this world. To that I respond that I truly believe Otto will learn whatever is essential when he is motivated to do so, because he sees the value in having that knowledge, and once learned, he will retain the information because it has meaning for him. After fourteen years of this approach, these ideas are no longer theory for us. We see them proving themselves again and again. For example, when he started doing more complicated math equations he saw the value of memorizing the multiplication tables, set his mind to the task, and committed it to memory over the course of three days.

I know we are all looking for ways to do right by our children. I hope that in sharing our approach, other people might find an element that speaks to them and it will help them along their paths.

Doug, Melissa, and Otto share a close family moment atop Haleakala, Hawaii's largest dormant volcano.

From Adrienne S. Poremba, mother of Alex and Georgia Pinsky:

My personal memories of elementary school include many moments of sheer panic. I didn't want my children going through the peer pressure and threatening atmosphere that exists there. Also, I didn't want my children to replace the respect they had for us as their parents with learned apathy that catches on like a virus amongst children that are shuffled off to concrete zoos.

When it became clear that keeping our children at home and educating them in the safety and comfort there was possible, we as parents seized this blessed opportunity to be with our children. We had a home business all the time our children were growing up. For the first decade, we had a stained glass studio and then, for the next eleven years, an alternative community-oriented newspaper. Alex and Georgia's time was, for the most part, their own. They listened to their internal clock. Mornings were a celebration, a time to embrace the coming day with enthusiasm. No tests, no fights, no disappointments.

Since they were not regimented and locked up inside a school building, they instead got to go for long walks in the Koʻolau Forest, listening to the birds, running through the sunlight that streaked through the tall eucalyptus trees, smelling the sweet aroma of yellow ginger, swimming in the picturesque waterfalls, snorkeling at the beach, or learning to surf, skateboard, and in-line skate. We wanted our children to experience life on its own natural terms, experience growing up like a human being, not a number in a system.

We socialized with a group of other homeschooling families and did many field trips together over the years. Also, camping, learning crafts, observing holidays, and celebrating family traditions were a core part of our network. [Our children] grew up in this special "ohana" [family in Hawaiian] of homeschoolers.

Every year was different. One year we hired a tutor for reading and math and brought the children to her for a couple hours at a time. Piano, ballet, martial arts, gymnastics, and horseback riding lessons were also an important part of their curriculum.

Another year, we collaborated with other homeschoolers and had tutors come to our property, and several families split the cost of the teachers' pay. We were fortunate to have built a wooden racquetball court where we held these classes, and afterwards the kids could all have fun bouncing basketballs, running around, and joyfully releasing their energies.

We did quite a bit of gardening in those days, and the kids learned to grow corn, potatoes, [and] tropical flowers, build tree houses, and bake bread.

Farm animals were a part of the daily routine to instill a sense of responsibility. Tending to the horses, taking care of the chickens, dogs, and baby calves were jobs that had to be performed and they loved doing these things.

Ken, father of Georgia and Alex, teaches
Thumper and Janus about his chickens.

The walls of our house were lined with bookshelves. A popular excursion was going to the Friends of Library used bookstore. We did not have a television set until the kids were about thirteen and ten years old.

There was always something to be done on the newspaper, and our daughter caught on quickly when it came to office work. She answered the phone professionally, learned to make ads on the computer, and typeset the calendar section like a pro.

Our son apprenticed under his father and together they built houses, [and] did remodels and handyman work. He is very good with tools and now has construction skills that can and will help him for the rest of his life.

We chose to homeschool our children in part because we wanted them to have a sense of serenity. They were able to live a life that was relatively stress free in terms of outside pressure, with no television blaring at them with visions of murder and mayhem to intrude on their peaceful little souls. We were blessed to be able to live free and to love them as much as we could during those formative years.

Your children are yours to love. Take advantage of the unique opportunity bestowed on you and spend as much time as you can with them. Providing a loving environment, filled with interesting things to do, books and lessons, friends, and healthy food is a good start to a good life.

From Lanet Abrigo, homeschooling mother of three:

I am a proud homeschooling mother of three amazing children. My children are gifted musicians preparing to sell their music globally, certified marine naturalists who do amazing outreach and education programs, certified junior lifeguards, top-of-the-line spear fishermen, and, best of all, they are happy, healthy, respectful, and honorable. They have touched so many people's lives and are truly gifts to this earth.

Emily, Quinn, and Timi enjoy a homeschooler's
version of physical education.
On Wednesdays they teach music on the beach.

Our path to homeschooling began with a very dissatisfying experience with a private school. Sadly, this school was touted as one of the best preschool-through-intermediate schools in our state. Long story made short, they couldn't keep my children safe, let alone make them happy. Substantial bullying problems led me to become active on the school board. I watched in horror as my son spiraled into depression. All his life he'd been this happy, loving, bright child that everyone wanted to spend time with. Now he was just a shell of the boy I once knew.

I first learned about homeschooling as an option from a friend. She shared with me her choice of curriculum and told me, "Girl, all you have to do is read the lesson and have him do the corresponding activities they list." My husband was thrilled at the idea, but I was scared to death that I would fail him. Then I took a *long* look into his big, brown, heartbroken eyes and realized we had to try. How my arms ached to hold him every day when he was at school. And then there was the terror in my heart that he was always in danger; it was time to step out of the box.

Our first year, we used a boxed curriculum, which I followed to the letter. My son *loved* it, and I watched with a full heart as my little boy began to bloom. The following year, I began to use the same curriculum for my daughter. She loved having her own schoolwork to do while her big brother did his. But the next year, we realized that there was an awful lot of repetitive busywork, so we stepped out of the box once more.

Since then, we have used a variety of things to teach the children. But the thing they enjoy most is life learning. We follow our passions and find ways to learn and be involved in the community through them. For example, the children play music at a local nursing home once a month. This connects them to reality and allows them to develop social bonds with people of all ages. The result is that my children are just as comfortable talking to adults as they are to other children. There is no social breakdown between the ages—it's all continuous.

My son is now twelve years old and has almost completed a high school general education course I purchased for him online. He teaches others how to surf, fish, and play music, which he does himself, at master levels. My daughter, now nine, is two full grade levels above her school-age peers. She's also the youngest certified junior lifeguard in our county. She holds the highest score on the written phase of the program, which is usually only offered for children ages eleven to fifteen. This put her above our county's top school children six years older than she. My youngest is five. He is an avid spear fisherman, fisherman, and educator about our oceans. He shares his passion of conservation and preservation like his brother and sister. Already years ahead of his school-age peers, he's yet another miracle in my life.

The *Abrigo 'Ohana* tuning up their instruments
before taking the stage for a concert.
www.abrigoohana.com.

I've realized there is *no* limit to my children's potential, and that anyone that tries to put a limit on them is not someone we need to spend time with. They have proven time and again that our choice to homeschool was the right one. I only wish I had started it sooner. I hope that you too will realize the gifts that your children are. As for me, my days have been filled with love and gratitude for their being. They know that, and so do I.

Sixty-four Reasons Why We Homeschool

1. It's fun.

2. Children learn more, and so do parents.

3. Parents enjoy being with their children.

4. It brings families closer together.

5. Parents get to see their children learn, to see the "lights go on."

6. Homeschooled children score higher on the ACT than schooled children.[21]

7. Homeschooled children tend to have a higher self-concept.[22]

8. Homeschooled children tend to be more calm and peaceful.

9. Homeschooled children can form friendships with a wider variety of people of all ages and from a much larger area than their school district.

10. Homeschooled children are less subject to negative peer pressure.[23]

11. Families have more time to pursue their own interests.

12. Children have more time to be kids, to play, and be happy.

13. The curriculum can be tailored to children's interests, needs, and skills.

14. Lively children need not be treated with drugs, which have unwanted side effects,[24] but can instead find appropriate outlets for their exuberant energy levels.

15. Bad influences can be minimized.

16. Children get more hands-on experience.

17. The family's values can be taught.

18. Children can progress at their own rate.

19. Children's questions and needs get more attention.

20. Children are taught by people who know them intimately and who love them.

21. Subjects can be studied in an order and at an appropriate age for each individual child.

Otto experiments with sculpting limestone.

22. Children who are socialized primarily by their parents, rather than by other children, tend to exhibit more positive social characteristics.[25]

23. Families can be in control of their time schedules.

24. Children are less influenced by the latest fads or behaviors in a particular clique.

25. Children can be more active, and
    thus more fit and happy.

26. Children's diets can be kept more nutritious.

27. The family need not endure hectic
    morning rushes to school.

28. Families' evenings need not be dominated by
    homework and mandatory early bedtimes.

29. Boring textbooks, boring workbooks, and boring
    assignments can be completely eliminated.

30. There is more time for reading
    fascinating real-life stories.

31. Learning opportunities can be seized
    upon when and where they occur.

32. Children experience more of the real
    world outside classroom walls.

33. Families can take vacations and go to
    beaches, parks, museums, etc., while
    other children are in school.

34. More learning can be done in less time.

35. Children with special needs can get more attention.

36. Children who are fast learners are not held back or
    occupied with busywork while the rest catch up.

37. Children have more time to explore their
    own culture, religion, and race.

38. Families are less subject to the political
    agendas of governments.

39. Cooperation can be stressed rather than so much emphasis being placed on competition.

40. Children can be motivated by their own interests and love of learning instead of by gold stars, grades, or threats.

41. Children can avoid being ranked, judged, labeled, and categorized, leaving more options open to them.

42. The family is likely to be stronger as a unit, which makes for a stronger community.[26]

43. Parents know from direct observation what and how well their children are learning.

44. Inaccurate tests, and thus false pride and unwarranted humiliation, can be avoided.

45. Children never lose, or can rediscover, their love of learning.

46. Learning can be done in more fun ways—field trips, board games, projects, and apprenticeships.

47. Children have more time and opportunity to discover and pursue their interests and special talents.

48. Children can be more gradually (if at all) exposed to the teasing, fighting, bigotry, aggressiveness, fierce competitiveness, danger, and other discipline problems prevalent in schools.

49. Children can live real lives right now, rather than spending twelve or more years in a classroom.

50. Children can have more basic freedoms, like being able to eat when hungry, use the toilet without having to ask permission, and go to sleep when tired.

51. Children have more opportunity to tune in to their own inner truths so their consciences can be more fully developed.

52. Children have more opportunity to learn responsibility because they have more opportunities to exercise responsibility.

53. Teachers and tutors may be found who are compatible with children's needs and personality.

54. Children are less anxious at home and thus learn more easily.

55. Homeschooled children aren't as exposed to diseases or head lice.

56. There's more time for music, art, and science.

57. Gifted children can be challenged.

Pacific Whale Foundation class on ocean conservation and squid anatomy.

58. Late bloomers can be allowed to blossom in their own time.

59. Sensitive children need not become intimidated or hardened.

60. When children are hungry and in the middle of something, mom or dad can bring them a snack or they can make their own.

61. When children are immersed in learning or doing something, they will not be interrupted by a bell every hour telling them they have to go somewhere else and study something else.

62. Parents are with their children more, so they are more in the know about the latest fads and slang and can speak their language.

63. Children are right there to keep parents on the cutting edge of technology.

64. It's okay to laugh and have fun during class.

Chapter 2

How to Homeschool: The Basics

That's as heroic as you have to be with your kids—
you just have to be honest with them."
—Michael J. Fox

Answers to Commonly Asked Questions

Is homeschooling legal?

Homeschooling is legal in all fifty states. For the laws in your state, you can call the Department of Education, and they will mail you the most recent regulations.[27]

Most state laws are not difficult to understand or follow, and your understanding of them will help you remain legal while maximizing your freedom. I have found that school personnel often do not know the laws and will attempt to enforce policies that are not required by law. Thus, it is important to be familiar with these laws yourself. See the last section of this chapter for some insight on how to negotiate the legal language of your laws.

Who can homeschool?

Enjoying being with your children is probably the most important thing! Ironically though, you will likely find, as we have, that the more you are with your children, the more you enjoy them. Other qualities that are helpful to have if you intend to homeschool are curiosity, playfulness, empathy, and respect for your children and their struggle. Humility is also an extremely important quality, as is a willingness to question your beliefs and learn from your children and your mistakes. And lastly, and maybe most importantly, a good memory helps—not for facts, but for what it was like to be your child's age.

On the flip side, some homes are so dysfunctional or intellectually impoverished that homeschooling would be difficult at best. For these families, school might provide children their best hope at rising above their family circumstances. That you are reading this book is probably proof itself that you are not in this category.

Won't my child fall behind?

The model of education as some sort of race up a hierarchical ladder is a convenient construct for mass education, but is not the only or best model for learning. Education is a lifelong pursuit; none of us will ever know more than a tiny fraction of what there is to know.

Homeschoolers have more freedom to choose what to emphasize in their education, but when they do follow a school's curriculum and are tested, they tend to outscore their schooled peers.[28] It's easy to underestimate the positive effect an observant parent can have in a loving family. According to the *Moore Foundation Bulletin*, "In a reasonably warm home, adult-child responses, which are the master key to education, will be 50 to 100 times more than the average teacher-child responses in the classroom."[29]

William Vitarelli, Ph.D., educator, architect, community organizer, peace activist, artist, grandfather, and loved by all who knew him, helps a youngster with her project. He passed away at age 99.
http://the.honoluluadvertiser.com/article/2010/
Jan/30/ln/hawaii1300336.html

Are there any well-known role models for homeschooling?

Many successful people were entirely homeschooled until college: Tim Tebow, Heisman Trophy winner and graduate of the University of Florida; Jason Taylor, 2006 NFL Defensive Player of the Year and the 2007 Walter Payton Man of the Year Award winner; pop music group, Hanson; and Christopher Paolini, best-selling author of the Eragon series. Erik Demaine, the youngest person to be hired as an associate professor of computer science at the

Massachusetts Institute of Technology, was homeschooled until he was fourteen and then entered college.

Many other well-known people went to school for varying amounts of time, but much or most of their real educations were achieved outside of schools. These people include Albert Einstein, Thomas Edison, Robert Frost, Sandra Day O'Connor, Leonardo da Vinci, and Abraham Lincoln.[30]

How do I get started?

I recommend that you sit down with your children and assess their interests and goals and your own resources. Chapter 3, What's Next?, will help you do this. Meanwhile, do the fun things together that you haven't been able to do because of the demands of school—go camping or to Disneyland on school days when there are no crowds, do projects around the house, read good literature, play games and sports, and spend time just talking. There will be plenty of time for formal study later. There is no need to rush.

How do I go about the daily work of teaching my child?

In most states, homeschoolers are pretty much free to follow whatever works for their own families, so how you go about your day depends on your beliefs about learning. On one end of the spectrum are families who believe in a school-like approach, with a teacher or tutors, assignments, regular hours, and such. These parents generally find it useful to purchase a formal curriculum. And in fact, most of us start out this way—partly because at first we're afraid to do it any other way.

On the other end of the spectrum are those who believe that children can't help but learn, and that life and play are their best teachers. These parents make themselves available to their children without insisting on any particular studies. The children in these families are sometimes referred to as "unschoolers." These parents are often not concerned with formal academics until their children are eight or ten or even older—whenever they are more mature and ready to tackle the physical and mental challenges of formal studies. They find these older kids can learn in months or weeks what it would've taken years to learn at an earlier age.[31]

Each family will find what balance of structure and spontaneity works best for them. Most parents will try to incorporate their child's interests into their curriculum, for there is no natural reason that we need to teach certain subjects at certain times. A child who seems only interested in video games, for example, might be fascinated with electronics, computer programming, or the history of video games (where they're made, how they're marketed, and more). This would involve reading and math and could expand out into virtually any subject eventually or perhaps a lucrative and satisfying career in video game design.

Then next month or year, they may suddenly want to study Shakespeare or oceanography with the same passion.[32] Thus begins a lifelong love of learning.

A simple chemistry experiment to establish whether a substance is a base or an acid.

Most of us start with some sort of formal curriculum and eventually evolve into our own programs. We all seem to end up using a variety of methods at one time or another.

You will find that opportunities for reading are endless; basic math can easily be taught by management of time and money and by cooking; and science is everywhere we look, plus there are many books with easy and fun science experiments using ordinary things found around the house. Virtually any knowledge can be found in the library, on the Internet, and among the people in your community.

What if there's a subject my child hates or just can't get?

Only in a classroom is this a problem. There, all children need to learn the same subjects at the same time or chaos results. Children who are too fast or too slow or just too cranky at the moment become enormous challenges for the teacher. At home we have far more options—we can move on to something new with the fast child, give the slower one extra help, or resolve crankiness with a change of activity, a snack, or a nap.

Furthermore, the subjects and schedules in school are set by people in another time and place. A child tired of reading for now but wanting to paint can't just go down the hall to the art room. As homeschooling parents, we need not conform to trying to create the generic lockstep education. We can tailor the day and any lessons to our child, his aptitudes, gifts, weak areas, mood, physical needs, and inspirations of the moment and quickly adapt to changes in any of these.

As I have written elsewhere, virtually all of us will do fine in life knowing the basics of a few subjects—how to read, manage our time and money, be a good citizen, and get along with others, for example. We specialize beyond that for our careers or for our own personal use and satisfaction, and this is often easier to do outside school walls or later in college or trade schools. Also realize that it is never too late to learn something if we later find a need for that knowledge or skill.

Marilyn vos Savant,[33] addressed this question in her weekly column in *Parade*:

Question: My 14-year-old son just does not get math. We have tried everything, including tutoring. He is a very visual and hands-on learner and is great on the computer. He also does well in English. But even when he really applies himself, he just cannot do math. Any suggestions? —J. Buchanan, Phoenix, Ariz.

Answer: If I were you, I'd forget about the math and concentrate on what your son can do well. Success is achieved by development of our strengths, not by elimination of our weaknesses. Name any successful person. Does this person have any weaknesses? You bet![34]

This is why we have accountants and bookkeepers, artists, plumbers, carpenters, lawyers, and doctors. In my own family, for example, my husband is great at anything involving his hands or numbers; I am the one who helps with words, meanings, and relationships. We need not be good at everything ourselves.

What if I'm not good at a subject my child wants to learn about?

This will happen and it's wonderful! You then have the excellent opportunity to teach your child how to find out about something neither of you know. You could look on the Internet or go to the library, find a tutor, or buy a correspondence course, for example. And a very under-publicized fringe benefit is that you get to learn new things, too. Parent-as-learner is surely the best role model of education a child can have.

Teenagers explore a mock paleontology dig to discover the ancient bones of a sea cow

But how will my child pass the tests she has to take?

First of all, read your laws carefully and consult with other homeschoolers in your state to make sure testing really is required. Our laws in Hawaii, for example, do give us the option of submitting something in lieu of tests, such as a video or a letter of recommendation from an adult outside the family. If testing is required in your state, you will likely have to "teach to the test" for a short period of time. Other homeschoolers or the school your child would otherwise be attending should be able to refer you to materials you would need.

But preparing for testing will go faster at home than in school because you'll have no distractions and can work on it when your student is well-fed and rested, and you can stop for breaks whenever you need to.

Here's what Einstein thought about tests: "One had to cram all this stuff into one's mind for the examinations, whether one liked it or not. This coercion had such a deterring effect on me that, after I had passed the final examination, I found the consideration of any scientific problems distasteful to me for an entire year."[35]

So reassure your child that tests are not a real measure of an education or intelligence. Give your child a chance to take a lot of practice tests so that her confidence is high at test time. Follow basic test-taking methods—make sure she sleeps well, eats a good breakfast, has her pencils sharpened, and arrives with plenty of time to spare. There are books that can add more, but that's all we did for our son's first test, a placement test for high school when he was sixteen. He studied for about six weeks, took the tests, and scored beyond the twelfth-grade level on English and math. This is just another example of how easy it is for a motivated student to learn in a short time what it takes captive children years to learn.

Don't stress and don't pressure your child. Do what you have to and then move on.

If I homeschool early grades, can my child go to high school?

A child homeschooled until high school may have to take a placement test before being admitted, as our son did. If this is the case for your child, find out what the test covers, and if the school doesn't have study materials, you can readily find them online. With a little bit of diligent study, passing the test should not be a difficult task.

A little-known fact about high school is that many states, like ours, have compulsory attendance laws, but do not say that a student must be working toward a diploma. When our son went to high school his junior year, he was not interested in a diploma from the school, so he picked his classes according to his own needs. He wanted to prove his mettle, so he took eleventh-grade world history and Japanese language. As a professional athlete, he felt more stage presence would help him in his career, so he took drama. He loves art and his high school had a first-rate art teacher , so he took art as well. He had a car, so he took auto mechanics.

While the school personnel were astounded by our request to do this, as it had never been done before, they acquiesced because they could find no law saying Thumper had to be working toward a diploma. Soon after our son enrolled, another homeschooled student did the same thing at another high school.

Personally, I believe that if schools allowed all of their students to follow their own needs and passions when selecting classes, somewhat like colleges do, most discipline problems would be eliminated and students would do better academically.

What about college?

College presents no real problem for homeschoolers. In fact some homeschoolers have found that their background works to their advantage as more and more colleges appreciate that they are often very self-directed and tend to excel academically. Homeschoolers have actually scored a half point *higher* on the ACT than all other test takers *every year* since 1997![36] In *Homeschooling for Excellence*, David and Miki Colfax describe how they homeschooled their sons. Three of them were at or had graduated from Harvard (their youngest was fifteen and still at home) when their book was published.

Some of the families in our group homeschooled early or middle grades, and their children went on to top-tier universities, and other children never went to any school until they went to college. College is just not an issue for a motivated learner.

Children roll out a sheet of clay at the studio of a local artist. Moana (left) has graduated from college, Mele is doing her student teaching and their younger sister is a junior in college. All were homeschooled their early grades. Thumper got a 3.8 G.P.A. in college courses before starting his videography business.

But remember, while a real *education* is invaluable, not all *schooling* produces a real education, and many careers require no document or degree—just a demonstration of competence. Often, too, the self-taught have a head start on those who spent four years in college. Recently a college grad from film school said he wished he could do what our son does for work. While that young man was hitting the books, our son was establishing himself as a freelance event videographer, and now is so in demand he sometimes has to hire others when he has two events on the same day.

Earlier I listed some successful homeschoolers, some of whom didn't go to college. There are also some very successful people who went to public school but didn't go to college or dropped out before finishing. To name a few: Steve Jobs, who dropped out of college after six months and went on to become co-founder of Apple Computers and Pixar Animation; billionaire David Geffen, co-founder of DreamWorks dropped out of college after his freshman year. He admitted, "I was a lousy student." Peter Jennings, news anchor, ABC's World News Tonight flunked the tenth grade and left high school at sixteen.[37]

What if my child has been labeled "learning disabled"?

Homeschooling families often find that their kids bloom and do far better at home and in the world-at-large than they did in school. Many of us feel that more than a few of the labels given to children are really more of a reflection of a school and how well it serves a child's learning style. If you look at your children's activities, you may see that they have far fewer problems learning about subjects of their own choosing at their own pace.

This is especially true of active children, usually boys, who may be labeled hyperactive in school because they can't bear extended sitting and book learning. Some children need breaks more often to get their bodies moving or to eat. In any case, involved and loving parents can see to it that their children get more personal attention at home than they could get in the classroom setting.

Furthermore, there is ample support for homeschooling special-needs children, as you will discover if you do a web search for this topic. Also see the resources section of this book.

If, after all this, you still feel your child needs professional help—and he is evaluated and meets the requirements for it—check your state laws. It is highly probable that you are entitled to these services as a homeschooler, and do not have to enroll your child in school to get them.

What about socialization?

As has been mentioned before, it is a myth that school is the best place to learn positive social behaviors. Remember, your child needs a variety of social experiences with diverse peoples, not just cliques and clubs and sports teams of his age-mates. The best of all social experiences is that of a loving family and extended family and the opportunities for lifetime connection that they can provide.

Won't my child get lonesome?

Perhaps, but so do schooled children. A discerning parent will know whether their child needs to be weaned from over-stimulation of other children and learn to entertain himself or whether he truly need more interaction with friends. If this is the case, there are many ways to develop friendships.

Pursuing interests like sports, dance, drama, art, music, etc., will result in contacts with people of all ages with similar interests. Boy Scouts and Girl Scouts, church youth groups, community center programs, and 4-H are other options. Make your home a friendly welcoming place where children want to come play and hang out.

Go on homeschool field trips with a local homeschool group. In many areas, there are classes during the day open to homeschoolers on everything from art and gymnastics to playing music and more. There's so much opportunity for interaction with other people that you may find you really look forward to those days when it's just you and your children at home!

Two weeks after our son enrolled in school for the first time at age sixteen, other students asked him how he knew so many people when he had never gone to school before. Our feeling was that because he wasn't confined to classes with age-mates and school cliques, he was able to make friends of all ages, from many groups and geographic areas.

Won't my child get bored?

Sometimes. But boredom has gotten an undeserved bad reputation. It can be an excellent impetus for creativity. A child who is kept busy all the time by scheduled activities gets little chance to tune into his own inner voice.

Today's children are busier than ever with school, homework, and after-school activities, yet they also seem more discontent than ever, as evidenced by rising violence, pregnancy, and drug use. Perhaps what they really need is a chance to just daydream and think and decide what to do and to discover life's joys at their own pace.

And I'll bet you've heard your schooled child complain about boring school classes and materials.

Won't I go nuts if I'm home all the time with my kids?

You won't go nuts, and you won't stay home. Without the demands of a school schedule, you can go out, enjoy life, show your kids the world, do the things you've always wanted to do as a family, and pursue and share your own passions. Not only will you be happier, but you'll also set a positive example for your children. You'll find many places, from campgrounds and swimming holes to museums and libraries, are not crowded during school hours. Go to homeschool gatherings in your area for the fun of it. Trade off with other parents.

Most homeschooling families treasure the increased time together and the opportunity to grow and learn together. It seems it's when kids are gone all day in school that many parents lose touch with them and forget how to enjoy them and appreciate their fresh insights into life. Interestingly, a common comment from parents about their kids when they stop going to school is that they became more of a pleasure to be around. They find much of their friction with their children was centered around school: the hours, getting to school on time, getting homework done, grades, and issues with teachers and peers. Homeschooling gives parents and children abundant time to get reacquainted and to rediscover the love they felt in earlier times.

I am a single parent and have to work. How can I homeschool?

Many homeschooling parents find themselves in this situation and it does require some ingenuity. There may be a homeschool study group in your area that shares your educational philosophy. You might form a co-op with several other families in your situation, each family taking all the children one or two days a week. Some jobs are such that children can go to the workplace with their parent; this may be as educational as anything they might learn in school. Perhaps there is a relative or neighbor who could teach your child for money or for services.

Also, a whole new genre of homeschool support services has sprung up in response to this need.[38] These may provide grade assessments; teaching of a curriculum provided by the school or the parent; tutoring in the home, a center, or online; help with passing standardized tests; and even field trips.

What if my child doesn't want to learn what he's supposed to?

First, figure out what you think he or she is "supposed to do" and see where you got the idea. We are often reacting to our own fears of "doing it wrong" or of being different, but when we take a real look, we are likely to find our meddling creates more problems than it solves.

Do you think he or she is supposed to learn phonics in second grade? Addition in first grade? Indeed, any subject at some particular time? This is not so for homeschoolers. Your children can learn any subject whenever they are ready, and you will find they learn it *far* more easily on their own schedule than a timetable set by educational bureaucrats or to please your hand-wringing relatives. Readiness to learn is key to ease of learning.

If you are worried they will never be ready, you are not

alone; many of us have had those worries, too. Our son was a "late reader" by school standards, but now, as an adult, he reads far more, both fiction and nonfiction, than most of his schooled peers. He never developed the aversion to reading that comes from having been required to read whether he felt like it at the time or not. After seeing many examples, I have complete confidence that a child with involved parents will learn all that he needs to learn in order to function in the society in which he is born. A child born into a hunting family learns to hunt. A child born into a literate home becomes literate.

Do you think your child needs lessons or textbooks? They probably don't. Most children, when left to their own devices, will show or tell you when they are hungry or tired—likewise with they need to be taught. For the most part, though, children learn through play and exploration and do best when allowed to proceed at their own pace in an enriched environment with a caring adult nearby.

Certainly, if your child shows a need for structure, give it. Our son used to love having a checklist of what he was going to do that day or week. He picked the subjects, activity, and pace, and liked to be able to check things off as done. It gave him a sense of accomplishment.

Furthermore, education is no different from the other activities of a family. What do you do when your child doesn't want to do chores? You might rethink your demands and see if they're fair or appropriate—maybe there's some other activity or subject more suited to your child. Maybe it's a matter of timing and another time of the day, another week, or another year might be better. Maybe your child is hungry or needs exercise or rest or some time in nature. Maybe it's your agenda for your child that needs examination, and your child has some other ideas that need to be heard. A more democratic approach to these kinds of conflicts is often helpful.

Children who were in school before turning to homeschooling seem to need some time to get school out of their systems. Schooled children are accustomed to adults telling them what is important to know and do. It may take weeks or even months until your child rediscovers his natural desire to learn, the drive that he had when he learned the complex skills of walking and talking without formal lessons. This is especially a challenge for a parent when it seems their child is just "doing nothing." But once your child has been given the space to own his life again, you can expect to find he has new zest for learning and is more open to your suggestions.

During this transition, some children do well when parents provide structure, while some do better when allowed to make their own choices. You'll work with your child to arrive at solutions you can both live with. There is no right or wrong way, and working out these issues may be an even more important learning experience—for both of you—than anything you might cover in a curriculum later. And it would be difficult to overemphasize the importance of thinking for yourself in these days of indoctrination that says we should follow the herd.

I suppose I should say that there are parents who just can't let go of the idea that they should be doing homeschooling in a certain way. These are mostly parents who are either afraid of doing it wrong or parents who are convinced they know best what, when, or how their child should be learning and they aren't going to question themselves. These parents may end up fighting with their children over schoolwork. In cases like this, if parents can't bring themselves to respect their child's views as valid and can't work out the conflicts in a win-win manner, it might be in the interests of everyone to try something else—help from another homeschooling family, a tutor or tutoring agency, or a charter school. And yes, a parent may send their child to school where they may be subdued or may still fight—but with teachers rather than parents.[39]

But I still have doubts.

And well you should! Consider my situation: I homeschooled our son all but a year and a half of his time from kindergarten through twelfth grade. I founded a homeschool support group. I've written lots of articles published locally and nationally. I've counseled countless parents regarding problems with their kids and with school officials. I've done battle with the state superintendent of schools. I've given homeschool lectures and seminars. And I've had doubts and fears regularly, and still sometimes do, I even wrote an article titled, "I, too, Cry in the Night."[40]

I have come to accept that doubts are an integral part of homeschooling and parenting, of life itself, and not just for those of us on the road less traveled. Parents whose children go to school worry about their children, whether they are safe in school, and they wonder if they should be doing something differently. Only the arrogant have the luxury of always being certain that their way is the only true way.

The rest of us will all, to some degree, question our choices, and for that, we can be grateful. Painful though it may seem at times, it is by questioning our beliefs that we can open doors to growth. Even our most cherished beliefs—indeed, especially our cherished beliefs—warrant regular examination to see if they really are true or if we are ready to outgrow them. We try to do the best we can with what we know and to accept that we will make mistakes. When we lose our way, special friends and family will understand and support us. We can consult books and magazine articles chronicling the lives of those who have been through the same trials that we are experiencing. And in the quiet of prayer or meditation, we may find that truth expresses itself.

Ultimately, we do not control the destinies of our children—nor should we. We learn to live with a certain level of doubt while doing the best we can and working to strengthen our faith in our efforts and in the children we are raising.

Overview of Basic Types of Curricula

Approaches to curricula boil down to three basic types. Any of these can be adapted to work with a schooled child. Most parents will end up using each of these at different times—or parts of each at the same time—as needs, interests, and perspectives change.

1. Curriculum designed by someone else.

2. Curriculum created by the parents, maybe with input from the children.

3. Curriculum provided by life and the serendipitous opportunities it presents.

Using a Curriculum Designed by Someone Else

Many new homeschoolers have found a formal curriculum to be a convenient and comforting way to make sure their children are learning what the children in public and private schools are learning. When the subject matter and methods match a child's interests and abilities closely enough, or a child is eager enough, this approach can work well.

These curricula are designed with the well-meaning intent of ensuring that all children will know all they need to know to be successful in life. The problem with this type of curriculum is that there doesn't seem to be a "standardized" approach that works with all children all the time—or even one child all the time. At these times parents may find it necessary to resort to using contrived methods to motivate their children. The risk here is that the intrinsic value of education can be degraded into learning for the sake of getting rewards (grades, money, and praise) or avoiding punishment. Struggles may ensue or the child may become a passive learner.

The costs of packaged curricula can be a disadvantage as they can be quite pricey. Some public school systems offer free homeschool programs, but I urge caution trying this. You may find this is the worst of both worlds—you do all the work with little flexibility, your child has no classmates, and you have the government in your home. Charter schools seem to do packaged curricula better by providing group activities periodically and by helping parents with the homeschool program. What to study and how to measure progress, however, are generally still out of your hands.

Homeschool support agencies can provide teaching for a standard curricula or one provided by a parent. They offer more flexibility and may be a good place to start for the parent afraid of going it alone or for the parent who has tried doing it herself but has not been able to work well with her child. The costs and services of these agencies vary.

Online programs or packaged DVDs can provide an interactive experience for children who enjoy computers. These curricula often keep track of progress making any reports required by the state easy for the parents to do. As long as these are balanced with a healthy dose of outdoors, physical activities, social interaction, creative pursuits, and meaningful work in the family unit, they can be excellent ways to provide a basic academic education.

The advantages of using formal curricula are that they provide a simple place to start and are often designed for self-study, an important convenience for a busy parent. Whatever else is being done in a day, there can be no complaints of "nothing to do." The curriculum alone may work fine for you, or it can provide a jumping-off point to help you gain confidence. If one doesn't work out, you will have learned something about what doesn't work with your child and why and will be better informed as you go on and try another packaged curriculum or another approach. Don't be afraid to experiment and depart from the day's plans when unexpected opportunities for learning arise.

As Rousseau cautioned:

> "A preoccupation with the skills the
> child will need in the future
> can blind us to the experiences the child
> needs at his or her present stage."

Drawing Up Your Own Curriculum—
Or Having Your Children Design It Themselves

Some families use a purchased curriculum and modify it to meet their own needs. Or they may just write their own from scratch. Or a child might write the curriculum based on his goals for the next year. (Samples of our parent- and child-written curricula follow this section.)

A curriculum can be as formal or informal as you choose. You already have experience with informal curricula. For example, when your child was a toddler, you would note his interests and design activities around them. I used to make a little list of things Thumper and I might do: play with toys, go to the library, watch big machines at work, read, go to the beach, and visit a friend. I'd then ask Thumper if he wanted to do any of these activities or if he had some other idea of how he wanted to spend the day.

Later, I simply set the house up with areas—clay always out on the clay table, books always in view, a craft or two on the coffee table, and various games, manipulatives, and imaginative toys clearly visible in boxes on shelves. Thumper would just gravitate to what he was interested in doing.[41] Alternatively, I would propose some ideas of things we might do to take advantage of the almost endless opportunities to learn and do things in the world at large, or Thumper might come up with some idea of what he wanted to do. That's one of the things I loved about homeschooling—the endless variety of activities, done with one of the most special people in my life.

The librarians at our local public library came to know us well, as we would go there weekly and grab books about pretty much anything and everything. These would be available like food at a buffet—to pick from according to our appetites at the time. We always included books on the outdoors and crafts in our stack, as we both loved these. Some had really cool and easy science experiments to do using items found around the house. We'd take heavily laden boxes of books home each week. Thank goodness Thumper got into chapter books when he got older, and I could just bring home two or three books at a time.

Eleven-year-old Alioune and his mother
learn about sharks in a public library.

On the other hand, as he came to his mid-teens, we used a more formal approach for his curricula. He had so many goals we needed to write them down at the beginning of the school year and use that as a guide throughout the year. He wrote his own curricula for the ninth and twelfth grades.

The assessments in chapter 3 will help you design educational activities that fit your family's and your interests and resources.

Learning What Life Presents Without a Specific Plan
Not using a formal curriculum is generally referred to as "unschooling" or "growing without schooling." One

generally starts with what a child is passionate about and helps her do that.

This is the "What do you want to do today?" approach or even the beneficent neglect approach—you just go about your life and let your child go about hers as nearby or far as is age appropriate. An observant parent can be alert for opportunities to extend her child's learning and provide other materials or experiences directly or tangentially related to a chosen subject. Though keep in mind that a little of this goes a long way, and too much can take the fun out of any playful activity.

While I am not necessarily advocating a complete hands-off approach, I think there is much truth in this quote by Ralph Waldo Emerson:

"Respect the child. Be not too much his parent."

Examples of Curricula We Used

The curricula below represent our goals for a particular year or years. Much learning took place beyond these and flowed naturally from our lives. These are presented only as a snapshot of our family's plans for a particular time. It happened that our son ended up being passionate about being a professional athlete (he has been ranked in the top ten and as high as fourth worldwide ever since turning pro in 2002). Your child may be passionate about being a doctor or a boat captain or a ballet dancer or a musician, and thus your curricula may look completely different from ours.

I hope our examples will stir your thinking to see how you might accommodate your child's talents into your program.

Kindergarten–Third Grade

This curriculum, being the first I wrote, was prefaced with several pages of description of our homeschooling philosophy. At that time, homeschooling was a novelty and to delay academics was nearly unheard of in most mainstream circles. I wanted to make it clear that even though we were not concerned with the traditional school subjects at this age, we were highly dedicated to what we felt was important to learn at this early age and that it was based on the research mentioned throughout this book. We now observe these traits in our son.

A. Positive Socialization and Social Responsibility

Cares for others and takes responsibility for their welfare; is friendly and kind; has good manners; contributes to the goals of groups to which he belongs; is fair and honest in his dealings with others; cares for plants and animals and helps preserve the environment; and contributes to making this a better world, especially by engaging in volunteer work without expectation of personal gain.

B. Intellectual Development

Maintains his natural curiosity, concentration, and love of learning; has a love of books and a wide vocabulary; understands that the purpose of reading, writing, and talking is communication; has math ability commensurate with his need; is extroverted and confident in his ability to find answers to his questions; and has expanding knowledge of the world at large and of the various laws that govern its functions, political and physical.

C. Values and Character Development

Has a high level of integrity; is cooperative yet stands up for his own beliefs; knows he is a loved member of a fully functional family; learns important lessons, such as that strength does not need to mean aggression, that bad actions do not necessarily mean bad people, and that peace begins with each of us; learns positive lessons from his father and other males about what it is to be a male and a father; understands the interrelatedness of life; is free of prejudice and has the courage to stand up to peer pressure; and learns our religious/philosophical beliefs and is respectful of the beliefs of others.

D. Physical Development

Is physically fit; knows and applies rules of good health, such as proper nutrition, exercise, stress management, sleep, and fresh air; cares for his body without catering to it unnecessarily; is aware of and can avoid dangers such as drugs, alcohol, and STDs; and enjoys participating in a variety of sports for fun and exercise, and not just because of the competition.

E. Self-Sufficiency

Understands the various machines and appliances in his environment and achieves competence in their use; contributes to the family by doing chores commensurate with his ability; takes care of his own needs, such as making his own meals and cleaning up after himself; uses his homemade phone book (with pictures of each person beside the names and numbers) to call up friends or entertains himself without adults, TV, or video games; understands from firsthand experience the relationship of work to the accomplishment of one's goals; and observes a wide variety of occupations and possible careers.

F. Emotional Development

Is playful, has a good sense of humor, and knows how to have fun without harm to himself or others; has observed and participated in disputes and learned how to negotiate to resolve them to a win-win end; is loved and loving; learns how to deal with emotions such as anger and grief; and has his self-trust intact, is aware of the strength of the force for good in the world, and energetically engages in "life, liberty, and the pursuit of happiness."

G. Aesthetic Sense

Enjoys numerous types of art, music, and dancing, both as a spectator and as a participant; enjoys the theater (as in plays, not just movies); cares for his possessions and his appearance; appreciates the peace and beauty of nature; and is creative.

Sixth Grade

By this time, Thumper had clearer goals and interests of his own. While we continued to bring home loads of library books on all subjects and to expose him to things we felt were important or interesting, he had

Using a drill to make a wind chime for Mom in the workshop of another homeschooling family.

many things he wanted to learn how to do. He wrote this curriculum and at the end of the year he actually gave himself grades on each item.

- Reading: aloud, making booklets, writing letters.
- Use appliances and tools (make list)
- Build stuff: fence, ramps, and other projects
- Sports: do strengthening, surfing, hiking, skating, bodyboarding, and gymnastics
- Work: wrap fish for my dad (at his fish wholesale company),make lollipops to sell, and build ramp
- Field trips: visit surfboard shaper
- Crafts
- Baking
- Survival skills
- Art: drawing and clay
- Science projects
- Typing

Ninth Grade

Thumper has now felt a need for more structure in order to focus on his priorities. He set this daily schedule when he was fifteen. He allowed for ample breaks and preparation time for the next activity and as always, used this as a guide not as a rigid schedule every day. Again, he evaluated his progress for himself. Of course, I had been an active participant, so I had my own sense of his accomplishments.

- 8:00 a.m.–9:00 a.m.: Breakfast, reading, and chores
- 9:15 a.m.–10:00 a.m.: Grammar
- 10:15 a.m.–10:30 a.m.: Handwriting
- 10:45 a.m.–11:45 a.m.: Spelling and vocabulary
- 11:45 a.m.–Noon: Journal
- Noon–1:00 p.m.: Lunch
- 1:00 p.m.–2:30 p.m.: Writing book on skating
- 3:30 p.m.–6:00 p.m.: Skating
- 6:30 p.m.–8:00 p.m.: TV and dinner
- 8:00 p.m.–9:30 p.m.: Reading, Scrabble, and dictionary game
- 9:30 p.m.–10:00 p.m.: Horseplay and getting ready for bed
- 10:15 p.m.: Lights out

Eleventh Grade

All these years, Thumper had been hearing about school from me and from his friends. His only experience had been the tour he'd taken when he was thirteen. We had some family discussions about whether his education would be complete without at least some experience in actually attending school. He decided to take another tour with a friend and, after that, opted to enroll. He did very well, earning a 3.8 grade point average and becoming a favorite of the teachers. He made some new friends, but he got bored and tired of the slow pace of learning and of so much time spent waiting for disruptive students to quiet down. He had always intended to get his GED, so he left school to work on that and on his other goals. He was glad he had gone to school, he enjoyed some of his classes, and had once again seen that he measured up to his peers.

Incidentally, when he studied for his GED, he again was focused and self-disciplined, just as he had been with his placement tests to go into school, where after three months of study, he scored twelfth grade plus on reading and math. For his GED, he learned things he will probably never use again (quadratic equations, for example), because he was determined to do the best he could. This is another example of how a child will do what is needed when he has his own goals to meet.

Twelfth Grade

Thumper's desire for more and more practical skills in his preparation for being on his own as an adult is clear in this curriculum he wrote for twelfth grade, and his range of interests continued to expand. Some of these goals were accomplished, some have become on-going as part of his life, and some, like guitar, were postponed for a future, more leisurely time of life.

- Business
  - ❏ Learn more about Dad's fish wholesale company
  - ❏ Learn how to cover for Dad if he's not feeling well
  - ❏ Learn how each employee's job works
  - ❏ Learn technical info like taxes, rent, overhead, and other accounting information

- Guitar
  - ❏ Learn all or most of the chords and get to the point where I can teach myself songs and read tab

- Break-dance
  - ❑ Learn Pop, Up Rock, Shoulder Roll, and Flares

- Gymnastics
  - ❑ Learn back handsprings, back flips, and misty flips on ground
  - ❑ Improve handstands and trampoline abilities: front Rudy, back Rudy, etc.

- Video Editing
  - ❑ Learn the complex programs: Final Cut, Premiere, and perhaps After Effects
  - ❑ Put out high-quality videos.

- Photography
  - ❑ Learn about exposure, lighting, angles, and effects with both video and photo cameras

- Self Defense
  - ❑ Learn basic techniques
  - ❑ Improve form
  - ❑ Learn some forms
  - ❑ Spar with Dad
  - ❑ Learn throws and street fighting safety

- Cooking
  - ❑ Learn how to cook my own meals: rice, veggies, meats, pastas, and more complex dishes

- Sewing

  ❏ Learn how to patch and hem my clothes

- Guns

  ❏ Learn how to use a rifle

- Auto Mechanics

  ❏ Learn more about cars

Jordan helps his son trouble-shoot his first car.

Examples of Learning Without Using a Curriculum

The curricula above are the structured ones we actually wrote down and loosely followed. Our primary method, however, was unschooling. Learning was very fluid, sometimes written as a to-do list and very structured down to the half-hour time segments and at other times completely spontaneous, taking advantage of whatever opportunities the day provided. Which plan we'd follow was determined by a number of factors: our travel plans, the weather, the surf conditions, what we were in the mood for, and what work we felt we needed to get done.

Our Not-Back-To-School Education

This is an example of a family trip causing us to set aside our planned curriculum in favor of using the travel experiences to broaden a child's experience. By simply making plans to do some interesting and productive activities plus allowing for spontaneous fun, we find we've got an enriching curriculum for a couple of weeks and the possibility of stimulating some new interests beyond that. Thumper was ten at the time, and I wrote this for the homeschool newspaper I was co-editor of along with Ken Pinsky.

Our first stop is California to visit friends for a couple of days. While there, we plan to visit some retail outlets to get them to sell our line of milk covers[42]—especially the Maui Dragon series designed by Thumper and printed by a company we found who did a good job at a reasonable price. Count this as geography and business administration.

After that, we'll be in Michigan visiting family. One of our favorite spots there is the university's museum of natural history, so we'll again tour that. Put anthropology and sociology on our curriculum.

We'll also be watching the UM Wolverines football team on national TV. We expect to see them win over Notre Dame. We'll then be there in person when they (hopefully) trounce Houston. The excitement and pomp of Michigan football and its halftime show, with the largest attendance of any college or professional sport in the United States, is an experience not to be forgotten. Add sports, music, and pageantry to our curriculum.

Of course, it'll be fall when we are there, and we'll be helping my folks rake the many leaves from the two kinds of oaks growing in their yard. We'll also experience the different weather of that latitude and season, as we have on our other visits during winter, spring, and summer. Chalk up credit for community service, botany, and geography.

Another favorite spot of ours is the Hands-On Museum, which has four floors of fun activities illustrating various scientific principles. There's some physics, chemistry, anatomy, and logic.

We will be searching though the university archives to locate a current address for a distant relative of ours, so add genealogy and research methods to our list.

Ann Arbor and the outlying areas were formed by glaciers that scoured the area long ago and left rivers and lakes. We'll be hiking and biking on trails around these areas. We'll be on the lookout for Indian fossils and poison ivy! There's more sports and botany plus geology.

As always, we'll be reading some great books (literature), and we will squeeze in a trip to Greenfield Village and the Henry Ford Museum. They have an unbelievably abundant amount of items of historical interest: Thomas Edison's laboratory, just as it was when he worked in it; the chair Lincoln was in when he was shot and the courtroom where he first practiced law; the first cars; the Spirit of St. Louis (the airplane that Charles Lindbergh flew on the first transatlantic flight); and much, much more. That's enough history for several years of curricula with a potential to spark an interest in so many diverse areas.

Flying home to Maui, crossing the mainland United States, is always interesting. This will be Thumper's eleventh trip to Michigan and each time we try to identify some landmarks in the terrain below. This year, we'll be on the lookout for the Mississippi and Missouri rivers as we've been following the flood coverage in *Newsweek*. There's more geography and some current events.

So, a simple vacation to visit friends and relatives with activities scheduled for the *fun* of it, provides us with real-life, hands-on history, geography, sociology, business administration, anthropology, sports, music, current events, math, community service, physics, research methods, literature, anatomy, logic, geology, and botany. Maybe we'll send you a postcard—oops, add writing to that curriculum!

Making a sculpture from driftwood
washed up by a recent storm.

A Day in the Life of an "Unschooler"

Perhaps it seems too easy to come up with learning experiences while traveling. What about an ordinary day?

How does unschooling work at home? Addressing that point, here is an article I wrote for national magazines: *Growing Without Schooling, Home Education Magazine,* and the *Maui Tropical Homeschooler (used by permission).*

Three years ago I wrote about Thumper's focus on marbles (also published in above magazines). He's twelve and I thought I'd write an update.

Now his passions are bodyboarding and rollerblading. A superficial look at our lives might lead one to conclude that we are just surf and skate bums. A closer look will reveal, however, that again, a passion for one thing ends up providing a well-rounded education. The rich variety of learning that results when "all we do is surf and skate" is, to my view, an unavoidable and enriching by-product of following our passions.

So here's a day I happened to pick to describe, as typical a day as any other.

We watched and discussed a bit of the OJ Simpson trial while we ate breakfast. This trial has been a real education in many fields for both of us as any who watched it will attest.

Then we called our surf contacts and the county weather report. They all said there were no waves, but we decided to check our favorite spot so we could confirm the accuracy of their reports. On the way over, I told him about an article I happened to read in the paper the day before, which I eventually read to him, about the ancient Hawaiians who used to live in the valley adjacent to this surf spot. Several fatal incidents had occurred between the Hawaiians and a trading ship that had anchored offshore. We talked about the bias of the author of the article because she had described the Hawaiians stealing of a boat and accidentally killing a ship's mate as a "bungled prank", rather than as a crime. There are ancient petroglyphs in that valley, to which we have hiked and now plan to see again.

We arrived at our surf spot to find that the reports were indeed accurate. We were surprised to find the wind blowing quite strongly onshore, because it had been blowing slightly onshore on the other side of the island, too. I knew and shared with Thumper the phenomenon of convection, the land heating up, causing the air to rise, creating onshore winds. We talked more about how the weather and the waves are related. We do know of certain aspects of the weather that accompany surf, so without looking at the ocean, we can tell whether or not there is surf somewhere on the island. Now we are working on a (secret) theory to even predict the direction of the surf. Remember, this is not a "Weather Unit" we're doing. We need to get accurate surf predictions because our favorite spot is a 40 minute drive away. Function is determining structure.

On the way back home, we noticed some whales so we pulled off at a lookout and watched through our binoculars for a while. Among the facts we've learned is some interesting trivia like: an adult whale's tongue can weigh 6000 pounds!

Resuming the drive, I asked Thumper's opinion about an incident during his last roller hockey game. Again, this was not some philosophy/ethics assignment. It was a real life problem. We discuss many things, and I truly value Thumper's opinion. The parents of the boy involved didn't want anything said about this to the league management or the coach. I was outraged by the incident and I felt the league president should know and that he should make the call as to what to do about it. Thumper's suggestion was that since we hadn't promised not to tell, we should tell the president the whole story, including the fact that the parents didn't want us to tell, but to not share with him our *feelings* about the matter. This struck me as incredibly wise advice, and we did exactly that with a very good outcome for everyone.

After getting home, we did our chores. One of his chores is to take care of the recyclables, taking them out to the garage and putting them in their respective bins and putting them curbside once a month to be picked up. I'm sure I need not elaborate on the knowledge he has acquired connected with this.

We then had lunch. As always, it was wholesome, and there's another body of knowledge he has acquired and applies in his daily life. In fact, I now learn from him, as he has taken nutrition to a higher level in his quest of excellence in his sport.

We watched the first half of the Michigan basketball game on TV. We're big Michigan fans and had been able to see the team play in a tournament here last October— during school hours. He got the autographs of the entire team and met the coaching staff and their wives and also got the autographs of the infamous Indiana coach, Bobbie Knight, and even Magic Johnson, who was watching the games. My dad always wanted to be a coach and sports writer... who knows how knowledge of sports will serve Thumper.

We set up the VCR to tape the second half and Thumper and I headed to the skate park. Last August, we had seen a demonstration by a roller-blading team called "Team 5-0" and had been awed by their skills and stunts. Thumper set himself a goal to be able to do stunts and to eventually be on a team. Since then, we have gone to the skatepark often and he has worked very hard at his sport there and in the street. As a result, he was recently invited to be a member of a stunt skate team of high-schoolers.

In seeking skating excellence, he has acquired another entire body of knowledge. He is an expert on the gear: skates, wheels, bearings, pads, helmets, and hockey gear. Another field that gets covered here is math: quarter- and half-pipes, vertical ramps, air spins of 180°, 360°, 540°, and 720° are all math concepts that he knows through personal experience. Then, too, one must make constant judgments of momentum, based on speed, his weight, and height when jumping obstacles such as stairs, where the consequence of being wrong is not simply a lower grade on a test, but a very real risk of bodily injury. We also figured in the factors of momentum when deciding whether he should get knee pads with one inch padding or the heavier 1 1/2 inch pads.

Further, he knows all the top skaters in the U.S., where they live, and what kind of gear they use. Actually, he is now one of those top skaters and is recognized most places he goes to skate.

He also knows similar information about the top bodyboarders in the world. We met most of them at the Rusty Pro Preliminaries a couple of months ago, again, during school hours. He knows much about many famous surf spots and has bodyboarded some of them himself. This is the history and geography that is important to him right now.

Incidentally, a couple of months ago, Thumper entered a bodyboarding contest in the novice division, all ages. He made the finals, where he competed with boys 14 years old and a 22 year old man, all of whom were a great deal bigger than he. In 6—8 foot surf, he had the highest points per wave, but took a very close 3rd because he had one less wave than the top two. He has considered a career as a professional bodyboarder, though he has decided to drop contests for now as they take the fun out of the sport for him.

Now the point of this is not to brag about his skating and bodyboarding, but to highlight that when a child is free to choose what he does with his life and time, he can find those things which inspire him to work hard, to overcome the inevitable frustrations and plateaus and to acquire the knowledge and skills needed to succeed. I know that he has the ability to set a goal and to do whatever is necessary to achieve it. Whatever subjects he decides he wants or needs to learn in the future, I have absolutely no doubts that he'll succeed at those, too.

So...back to the skatepark. We spent an hour there skating and socializing, and then we and some friends headed over to the tennis courts of Maui High School to play hockey, as we have often done. This time, however, the security guard told us someone had broken his arm there and was now suing, and so they weren't letting anyone skate there anymore. We got back in the car and headed back to the skate park, discussing on the way the problems of civil suits and personal responsibility and how Congress had promised reform of this area. Naturally, other events have prompted discussions of national and international politics, too.

When we got to the skate park, it had started raining, so we came home. Thumper set to work with the cordless drill changing the wheels on his skates and taking off his grind plates as he had hockey the next day.

After dinner, he helped clear the table and then he read to me, something he enjoys doing very much. When we went to bed, I read to him.

There it is—just a typical day of checking the surf and going skating, with a little history, geography, math, science, ethics, law, reading, physics, meteorology, socializing, political science, and current events happening along the way, *none* of it planned.

I've concluded that learning facts takes care of itself when we can choose our pursuits. Our interests have resulted in our exploring our unique place in the universe: we've hiked deep in our jungle valleys, swum under glistening waterfalls; we've been at the top of our mountains and down into volcanic craters; we've skated parks and sidewalks, schools and historical spots; we've spent whole days bodyboarding, one day seeing a pod of whales swimming closer to us than we were to the shore. We've observed the tides, the phases of the moon, the winds, the clouds, and the moods of the sea. We've been on hundreds of field trips and have indulged in art exhibits, theater, movies, and computer games. We've made an abundance of gifts and have done many science projects. We've done volunteer work and have visited the elderly. We've made friends with people of both sexes, all races, all ages. We've read what interested us and spent our time on activities that matter to us, accompanied by the people we care about the most. We've done work that we saw the need for and we've helped each other in countless ways both big and small. I feel that in pursuing our unique interests, we are acquiring knowledge that goes way beyond facts, wisdom that cannot be quantified.

Every individual in this huge diverse world of ours has his own niche, the place where he fits, belongs, where he feels inspired and cherished. When he is free to discover and explore his, as we have been ours, his roots will go deep and his life cannot help but flourish.

Greeting the sunrise at the summit of
Haleakala before making the 11.2 mile hike
through the Crater with family and friends.

Using the Internet for Homeschooling

For the new homeschooling parents of today, this chapter is probably not needed. Your children were born into a wired world and are likely fully computer literate. That's not how it was in the "olden days" of the nineties! We spent a bundle on a beautiful encyclopedia set that was out-of-date by the time it arrived. While we did enjoy sitting at the kitchen table looking up articles and pictures of interest, we were limited to the point of view presented by the authors of the encyclopedia entries.

We also checked many books out of the library and these were better, as they presented myriad points of view. We used a few workbooks and learned much firsthand from the people who were doing the things we wanted to learn about. For example, when our son was about eight, and again a couple of years later, our homeschool group had a science tour at our community college, replete with all sorts of experiments presented by the department head.

Of course, these options are also available to you. But now, at the click of a mouse, you can also easily access virtually all the world's knowledge, complete with graphics, video, and links: unit studies; subject studies; entire curricula for any and all grades; secular, religious, Waldorf-based, Montessori, certified, and uncertified programs; programs that come with monitoring by teachers; some self-monitored programs—the options are virtually endless.

With parental controls and supervision, you can ensure the materials your children have access to are appropriate for their developmental level, and you can protect them from sites that are inappropriate.

I sent out a request to current homeschoolers for a brief description of how they use the Internet. Here is the response of Nita Bowman. . My guess is that her use of the Internet for research and ideas is more typical of homeschoolers today, than working with a purchased or downloaded curriculum is.

"We have used the Internet for many educational things. I usually go to the web when I can't find what we are looking for in the books that we have on hand, like a list of prefixes and suffixes, the name of the seaweed we found at the beach, the name of the weird fungus we found in the yard, the name of the cool snakes we found in the garden, the correct solution to a math problem, different methods to study the times tables, info on a historical figure, etc. We also have found other useful things on the web, like great videos which explain complex things at a child's level, videos on the history of our banking system and what it is today, how consumerism works and how it is affecting the planet, how to make kombucha tea, how to sew with a leather tool. There are many web sites with free stuff for homeschoolers, like free worksheets, free pretests, free crafts to print up, free patterns, free newsletters, free homeschool ID cards, etc. We always use the Internet to check for books and videos in the local library before we go. Basically, we use the Internet for help in every school subject."

For online resources, see Appendix C.

Homeschooling and the Law

A fair amount of the calls I have had over the years from homeschoolers involve questions about demands that school officials make of parents. Almost always, these demands go beyond what is required by the law—mostly because the officials have not taken the time to know the laws.

In this section, I will cover some regulations from our state (Hawaii) as examples and discuss those problems or questions that typically come up. I will use them to illustrate what to watch out for in your own state laws. I caution the reader that I have no formal legal training and am not giving legal advice. What I have done, though, is studied our regulations thoroughly and have helped lobby for some of the revisions that we wanted. I also fought a winning battle with school officials all the way up to the state level, including the superintendent and the attorney general, when my county officials insisted our son had to jump through some hoops that the law did not require. Should you ever run into a real dead end with your local school officials, the counsel of a licensed attorney should be sought. You can find ones specializing in homeschool law online.

Homeschooling is legal in all states. Many states have excellent laws, allowing a great deal of freedom and yet sufficient oversight to satisfy the state's interest in seeing that children are not neglected. Other states make it more difficult, requiring a bit more creativity on the part of families to pursue their own programs. Take responsibility for learning your own laws.[43]

The most important thing you can do is thoroughly read and understand the words used in your educational laws. "May" does not mean "must," for example. It is also important to note what words are *not* used. In our state, we file a "notice of intent." No mention is ever made of "permission." Parents *notify* the school of their intent and then simply begin homeschooling.

Here is another example of how critical the precise meaning of a word can be: "The parent(s) submitting a notice to home school a child shall be responsible for the child's total educational program including athletics and other co-curricular activities."[44] If you look up "responsible" in the dictionary, it has such synonyms as "accountable," "answerable," "liable," and "chargeable." But when you look at "responsibility," it clarifies that this means, "the ability to act independently and make decisions."[45] Parents, in exercising their "responsibility," are thus able to decide for themselves what their child's total educational program is and to act upon their own decisions independent of any school officials' ideas or permissions. Homeschoolers are free to create and implement their own programs as they see fit.

On the other hand, there is nothing in these regulations that *forbids* schools from accepting homeschooled children into various classes or school sports. Just as responsible parents might enroll their children in classes not connected with any school, so too, might parents exercise their responsibility by enrolling their children in school sports, for example. If a school has requirements, such as good grades, for its students to be able to participate in these sports or extracurricular classes, then certainly they could require that homeschooling parents ensure that their students are performing well on their curricula. In many parts of the country, schools do this with no problems, while others balk at the idea of homeschooled children in their midst.

Another important regulation to look for in your laws is the one regarding school services, such as special education. Our law reads, "All educational and related services statutorily mandated shall be made available at the home public school site to home-schooled children who have been evaluated and certified as needing educational and related services and who request the services."[46] Find out if your state has a similar statute—which it likely does—and if the services of a speech therapist or other specialists are available to schooled children, your children are probably entitled to those services as homeschoolers.

Extreme caution is advised, however, because state and federal services always come with a hook. They will classify your children and often pressure you into sending them to school, as they tend to feel that homeschooling contributes to, or even causes, problems. Often, the opposite is true—a "special" kid may do better at home, where he feels the safest and most loved, and can have your personal attention without the distractions of other special-needs children.

What is *not* said is also a key element in this regulation: "The parent submitting a notice of intent to home school *shall keep a record* of the planned curriculum for the child. The curriculum shall be structured and based on educational objectives as well as the needs of the child, be cumulative and sequential, provide a range of up-to-date knowledge and needed skills, and take into account the interests, needs and abilities of the child."[47] Notice that the regulation does not say that the parents need to submit their curriculum to anyone, but that they shall *keep* it. It doesn't even say it has to be written down.

Your state may require testing, and if so, your children may be able to participate in testing along with schooled children, or you may find private groups who can do this. Our state allows us to submit an alternative to testing. We lobbied very hard to get this into our laws so we wouldn't have to be swept into the trap schools are in: having to teach to the test.

When it came time for our son to be tested in 1992, at the end of third grade, I requested that I be allowed to submit a video instead. My principal refused my request, and, to my amazement, so did the Maui District Office. So I appealed it all the way to the state superintendent of schools and other state officials. After much correspondence back and forth, they finally acquiesced and accepted my video. I've not had any problems since. My opinion is that they decided I was more bother than they wanted. For the sixth and eighth grade testing years, I simply sent a more detailed report of what we'd done and read and didn't hear a word from them. I have not heard of anyone having any problems since then.

One thing I learned from my engagement with the DOE over testing was the importance of not asking a question that could have an answer you aren't willing to accept. That is, don't ask, "May I submit a video (or whatever)?" School officials may answer as they did to me, "No." Instead, send it to them with a note saying it is your report in compliance with the law. They can reject it, but it's much more trouble for them, and your chances are good they won't want to bother.

There may still be some principal who insists on requirements beyond the law. If you run into this, be polite and calm and send him a copy of the regulations with the pertinent section highlighted. If he still refuses, appeal to your district office.

If the school is still uncooperative, John Holt, education reformer, author, and speaker, recommends that you insist that all communication with a school (or any other government agency) be in writing, and if it's over the phone, you take notes and repeat back information as necessary for confirmation.[48] Only as a last resort, go into the school. The school building is the school's territory, and you may be quite surprised at how intimidating it can be to be a parent trying to challenge a school official on his home turf. Arm yourself with knowledge if you must go into the school. Be well rested and well fed. Dress professionally, yet comfortably.

I once had to talk to a school counselor about a child I was mentoring. The child's parents were considering homeschooling, and the counselor was so sure she was right in her statement that this child had to be tested, that she searched her file cabinet in a somewhat huffy flurry, and finally pulled out the regulations to prove it to me. How embarrassed she was when she found out I was correct. But only my certainty enabled me to stand up to her insistence.

In most states, you will not get high school credits for your homeschooling efforts. But credits are really just chalk marks adding up to a high school diploma of dubious value. Homeschooled kids go on to get great jobs, have satisfying careers, and get into excellent colleges, including schools as exclusive as Harvard, without any of these credits and credentials.

If you feel your child needs a diploma, an accredited homeschool program can provide one, or she can get a GED through self-study or a tutoring service. The tests on the GED are norm referenced using the scores of a cross section of graduating high school seniors nationwide. The scores include a percentile ranking, and so can replace a grade point average. For example, if the schools in your state are not ranked in the top 10 percent, then a score on the test in the top tenth percentile could be seen as more valuable than all As in your school. The GED opens most doors available to high school graduates in the job market and public and private universities. Homeschoolers are very welcome at top-tier universities, including the Ivy Leagues, as the best schools want diversity and seek self-motivated students.

I hope these tips will help you when you study your own laws, and more help is available at the various web sites listed in appendix C at the end of this book.

Chapter 3

What Next?

> *"Whatever you can do or dream you can, begin it.*
> *Boldness has genius, power and magic in it."*
> —Johann Wolfgang von Goethe

The Best Place to Start: Where You Are!

It is easy to underestimate what a wealth of knowledge and skills you and your spouse have to share with your children, not to mention what can be learned from the aunts, uncles, grandparents, neighbors, best friends, and others in your community.

To help you discover more of your skills and knowledge, questionnaires are provided below.[49] The first is to help you learn more about your children, their personal and educational experiences, and opinions; the second leads you through examining your own beliefs about children and education; the third covers aptitudes and skills you have that you might share with your children; and the last one will help you set your strategy.

You might write out the answers to every single question below or none of them. But do take your time exploring the concepts and personal experiences to see what you can learn about yourself and your children. The more you know and understand about yourself and your children, the clearer your path will become.

Let's Go Treasure Hunting: The Questionnaires

About Your Children

Ideally, you will write out your own answers to these questions in a notebook to which you can refer and add to later and then have each of your children answer them. Set up a private space and assure your children that their answers will be between you and them. Help as needed with understanding the questions or asking other questions to get full answers, but don't evaluate or invalidate the answers or comment on them. Your role is to make it safe for your children to answer honestly. If you think you can't do this or that your children may not be completely frank with you, have someone else do it for you.

For you to answer and then have your child answer them, using his or her name for "your child"

Family

1. Who in your family does your child like to spend time with the most? Why?

2. Is there anyone in your family your child doesn't like to spend time with? Why?

3. Does your child have a favorite aunt? Why is she the favorite?

4. Does your child have a favorite uncle? Why is he the favorite?

5. Other supportive adults? How are they supportive?

School/education

1. How does your child like school? (If he is too young for school, substitute "being taught" for "school.")

2. What does your child like best about it? Least?

3. What do you think would have to change for your child to like it more?

4. What is your child's hardest subject? Why? Easiest subject?

5. What is your child's least favorite subject? Favorite?

6. How well does your child feel he is doing in reading (speed and comprehension), math, and language (spelling and grammar)?

7. For the hardest subjects, why does your child feel he is having problems?

Life

1. What are your child's hobbies? What would she like to do with her time?

2. What would your child like to know more about?

3. What would your child like to learn to do?

4. What would be a perfect week from your perspective? From your child's perspective?

5. What are your goals for your child?

What are her goals for herself?

6. If your child could change anything about her life, what would it be?

7. Who are your child's heroes? Her biggest fans? Her harshest critics?

8. What kind of person would your child like to be? What kind of person would you like her to be?

9. Do you feel your child is becoming more that kind of person as a result of school?

10. Is there something you feel your child would like to tell you, but doesn't feel safe doing so?

Ponder Points

1. Compare your answers with your child's. Did you learn anything about your child that you didn't know?

2. Were any of the answers your child gave a surprise to you? How do you feel about his/her responses?

A nature connection advocate helps boys find deer and raccoon tracks by a stream and make plaster casts of them.

Your Beliefs about Children and Learning

1. If given a choice, do children want to learn new things? What have you observed that supports this view?

2. Do you want to learn new things? Why or why not?

3. Is it important to have your own reason to learn something before setting out to learn it? Or is it better to have someone else tell you what you should learn?   Compare things you've learned on your own with things others decided you should learn. What do you notice?

4. What makes learning easy? Hard? Useful? Useless? Interesting? Boring? Try to think of examples from your own life.

5. How important is it to you to not stand out as different?

6. How important is it to you to have the same knowledge and skills as others your age? How important is it for children to have the same knowledge as their age-mates?

7. Do you trust children? Do you think they are eager to follow good role models?

8. Or do you think they are naughty and manipulative? How does your belief either way affect how you treat them? How might your beliefs and treatment affect how they act?

Your Abilities and Interests

1. Write down some things you are interested in

learning more about or learning how to do. List some ways you might learn about these.

2. Go over your child's answers in her self-evaluation and comb through them for anything that she wants to learn more about or learn how to do. Also, consider things like who her heroes are— whatever field the hero is in is an opportunity for knowledge. Even an answer describing a perfect week, "Every day at the beach," could be useful for all sorts of education: marine biology, weather, sculpture, and engineering sand castles, etc. Make a list of your answers.

3. What are some things you love to do that you would like to share with your child? Add those to your list.

4. Do you have friends or relatives with skills, trades, or knowledge that you don't have? Add them to your list.

5. Would any of the items on your list involve reading, writing, or math? If not, which is quite unlikely, how might you use the list to give your children practice in these areas?

Ponder Points

1. What thoughts do you have about your list? How would you feel if your child learned most of what is on the list?

2. What holes are there in making it a balanced curriculum?

3. How might you fill those?

Your Personal Resources for Homeschooling

1. If both you and your child's other parent were working, would you be able to arrange your schedules or sacrifice some income so that one or both of you could homeschool your child(ren)?

2. If you need both incomes, are there other ways you can make it work? Tutors? Co-ops? Could you bring your child to work with you? Could relatives help? Is your child old enough to be left home alone to work on his own?

3. Do you already know homeschool leaders/ groups in your area who offer support and connection with like-minded families?[50]

4. Do you enjoy your children's company?

5. How much structure does each of your children need? Does it vary? What makes it different from one time to another?

6. Are you willing to respond flexibly to the changing needs of your children?

7. Are you ready for some of the most fun, rewarding, and important work you will ever do?

Conclusion

There you have it, a guide to the "road less traveled." This road has become wider and better traveled over the last twenty years, with seasoned parents and grown homeschoolers along the way to give you a hand should you become worried or falter.

You have learned many of the reasons why we homeschool and various ways to go about it, including sample curricula. You have read firsthand accounts of our experiences, written both by parents and by children and young adults. You have had a chance to apply what you have read to your own experiences and to formulate ideas from them as a basis for personalized curricula for your children.

I hope you have learned that you are competent enough to take charge of the education of your children, and that you have recognized that even if your children stay in school, you can apply what you have learned here to better their educational experiences in the time you are with them.

In the appendixes that follow are some maxims and favorite quotes and a list of resources. Books, web sites, links to magazine articles, and just plain interesting sites are included there, with my favorites starred. Many of the web sites offer material for teaching just about anything.

But I must caution you: even a superficial Internet search will present you with an overwhelming number of programs, kits, and (mostly very long) books. You could come away feeling as if you are doing it all wrong if you aren't doing something like teaching your third grader Spanish or your sixth grader algebra. Hopefully this book has reassured you that it is fine to simply respond to the needs of your children as you see them right now. You might be setting your child up with a recycling business like five-year-old Kade's parents are doing; looking up the recipe for kombucha tea like Nita is doing with her three children; or teaching your older son about real estate, like Bob did. If there is a need for Spanish or algebra or any other subject, responding to that need will come naturally at that time, and the learning will proceed far more smoothly.

I suggest you start simply. Try to make your program personal to your life and the things that get you and your family excited. Every family has some unique experiences and knowledge that would be valuable to pass on its children. Once that part is established, add in other things that you and your children find interesting. As time goes on, your children will express the desire to study other subjects or to acquire other skills and those can be added in, too.

The supplies in an ordinary home and the public library really are all you need to get started. You just can't beat public libraries, not only for free books, but also for the assistance of their librarians and their great programs for children like puppet shows and storytellers.

Of course, check out the laws in your state. When we started out homeschooling, people would ask, "Is that legal?" and we ourselves worried about the school personnel's scrutiny. But after a few years, the schools had seen enough of the achievements of homeschoolers that they were actually referring parents to me. Folks in the community now say, "Oh, that is the best way!" Even my own brother, a retired middle school history teacher, came to say this about the homeschooling of his nephew.

Our son is now grown and independent, but I have kept active by writing, speaking, and doing phone consulting. I love hearing fearful parents light up as they get confident and excited to start homeschooling. I wrote this book in hopes it will do the same for you. I am always available to answer any particular questions. You can contact me through my web site:

www.HomeschoolingWhyandHow.com.

Good luck, enjoy your children, and be prepared to grow and learn right alongside them.

Mother and son enjoy a moment in the woods.

Father and son off to (hopefully) catch dinner!

Appendix A: Maxims for Parents

1. Your relationships with your children and others are paramount. No facts or tests matter as much.

2. Relax and recognize that none of us will ever know even a small fraction of the knowledge that would be useful to us.

3. Learn from your children. They have a fresh perspective.

4. Have fun with your children—it will make learning easier and your life happier.

5. Recognize that any subject may be valuable to your child.

6. Trust that when you child balks, he has a reason for doing so that makes sense to him. Find it, so you can do something helpful about it.

7. The Golden Rule is a great standard for evaluating your parenting and teaching methods.

8. Spend as much time as possible in the natural world.

9. The solution to academic problems may be physical—sleep, food, exercise, fresh air, change of pace, etc. If the problem doesn't resolve itself, it's not the problem. Keep looking.[51]

10. If you don't know what the words mean, you won't understand the ideas.[52]

11. If you are confused, you likely missed something earlier.[53]

12. If you are feeling dead or bored, chances are you need some real world experience with the subject or a break to do something more active.[54]

13. Education is a lifelong pursuit. Nothing
    has to be learned by a certain age
    unless the learner has need of it.

14. Knowing how to do things well has intrinsic value.
    Rewards and punishments pervert that value.

15. Listen more; talk less.

16. Religion, philosophy, and values are
    best taught by being lived.

17. Role modeling what to do when you don't know the
    answer is more important than knowing the answer.

18. Good character is a higher
    achievement than good grades.

19. Remember what it was like to be your child's
    age. It will make you more empathetic.

20. Keep doing your own homework—academic,
    parental, and religious/spiritual.

21. Often the answers are there for the looking...
    in the present moment rather than in a book.

22. The best solutions will be both intelligent *and* loving.

23. Don't take yourself or your thoughts too seriously.
    Instead laugh and be silly more often.

24. Relate to the best you can see in your child (and
    others). It is what is most true about them.

25. Don't be overly concerned about bad
    outside influences. They have far less influence
    than what goes on in the home.

26. Being real and genuine is far more
    important than being consistent.

27. Your needs matter, too. Negotiate.

28. Treat each "misbehavior" as a learning opportunity—for you and for your child.

29. Live by the Serenity Prayer: try to change what you can, accept what you can't, and know the difference between them.

30. Have faith. What may look awful now often turns out to be the best thing that ever happened.

Appendix B: Two Favorite Quotes

I am a quote collector and the web site for this book has a section of many of my favorites pertaining to parenting and homeschooling. Those quoted below, however, are just too basic and too important to leave to the chance the reader will go to the web site. In fact, the daughter of the author of "A Synopsis" expressed her hopes that the entire piece would be quoted in this book. These two now deceased educators, researchers, and writers have each been important pioneers in the homeschool movement. The late Dr. Moore describes his extensive research and the case for delaying school that he came to as a result.

Moore's educational career began as a teacher, principal, and superintendent of California public schools. The research he compiled about the effects of schooling on young children steered his career away from higher education and into homeschooling. Dr. Moore was the world's foremost expert witness on the topic of homeschooling, appearing in courts as far away as South Africa, West Germany, Great Britain, Japan, Australia, and New Zealand, as well as in Canada and the United States.[55]

The second quote is from John Holt, often described at "the father of homeschooling," started his career as a teacher but eventually gave up on the idea of reforming the schools. He spent the rest of his life researching learning methods and soon became a passionate champion of homeschooling, or learning all the time, as the book he was writing when he died is titled.[56]

While his books are also based on extensive research, I love this quote for its poetic language and for the light it shines on the love Holt had for children and the hope he had for improving their lives and education.

THE MOORE FOUNDATION...
A SYNOPSIS by Raymond S. Moore[57]

For more than 40 years some of us have been concerned that most children are surrendered by homes to institutional life before they are ready—with serious implications for the children, the family, society, nation and world, including economic and moral disaster. In the late 1960's following a stint at the U.S. Office of Education, I became convinced that our children were victims of dangerous trends toward earlier schooling. We had reasons to be skeptical of school claims for early academic achievement and socialization simply because "young children learn so fast." By giving our schools "green grain" for their mills, we make their task impossible. Although challenging conventional wisdom and practice was not a pleasant prospect, colleagues around the world have more and more given support to our research, some reversing historic positions to do so. We offer here a synopsis of our books (***Better Late Than Early***, ***Home-Grown Kids***, ***Home-Spun Schools***, and ***Home-Style Teaching*** and our monograph ***"Research and Common Sense"*** from Columbia University's ***Teachers College Record***, Winter 1982-83), and chapters in more than 30 college textbooks in various languages.

Our conclusions are actually quite old-fashioned. They seem new to some because they differ largely from, and often challenge, conventional practice. Our early childhood research grew out of experiences in the classroom with children who were misbehaving or not learning because they were not ready for formal schooling. Concerned first with **academic** achievement, we set out to determine the best ages for school entrance. But more important has been the **socialization** of young children—which also involves senses, coordination, brain development, reason, and social-emotional aspects of child development. These conclusions come from our Stanford, University of Colorado Medical School, Michigan State and Hewitt investigative teams who did basic research, and also analyzed more than 8,000 early childhood studies. We offer briefly here our conclusions which you can check against any sound research that you know (It is thoroughly documented in our book, ***School Can Wait***):

Readiness For Learning. Despite early excitement for school, many, if not most, early entrants (ages 4, 5, 6, etc.) are tired of school before they are out of the third or fourth grades—at about the ages and levels we found that they should be starting. Tufts University Psychologist David Elkind calls these pressured youngsters "burned out." They are far better off **wherever possible** waiting until ages 8 to 10 to start formal studies (at home or school)—in the second, third, fourth, or fifth grade. They then quickly pass early entrants in learning, behavior and sociability. Their vision, hearing and other senses are not ready for continuing formal programs of learning until at least age 8 or 9. When earlier care is absolutely necessary, it should be informal, warm and responsive like a good home, with a low adult-to-child ratio.

Using the board of the game, "Risk," to understand where Iraq is at the start of the first Gulf War.

The eyes of most children are permanently damaged before age 12. Neither the maturity of their delicate central nervous systems nor the "balancing" of the hemispheres of their brains, nor yet the insulation of their nerve pathways provide a basis for thoughtful learning before 8 or 9. The **integration** of these **maturity levels** (IML) comes for most between 8 and 10. It is not fair to test children for formal learning before at least age 10.

This coincides with the well-established findings of Jean Piaget and others that children cannot handle cause-and-affect reasoning in any consistent way before late 7's to middle 11's. **And the bright child is no exception.** So the 5's and 6's are subjected to dull rote learning which requires little thought, tires, frustrates and ruins motivation, stimulates few "hows" and "whys". Net results: frequent learning failure, delinquency. For example, little boys trail little girls about a year in maturity, yet are under the same school entrance laws. HEW figures show that boys are 3 or 4 to 1 more often learning disabled, 3 or 4 to 1 delinquent, and 9 to 1 acutely hyperactive. So, unknowing teachers far more often tag little boys as "naughty" or "dumb". And the labels frequently follow them through school.

Socialization. We later became convinced that little children are not only better taught at home than at school, but also better socialized by parental example and sharing than by other little children. This idea was fed by many researchers from Tufts, Cornell, Stanford and California. Among the more prominent were (1) Urie Bronfenbrenner who found that at least up to the sixth grade, children who spend less of their elective time with their parents than their peers tend to become peer-dependent; and (2) Albert Bandura who noted that this tendency has in recent years moved down to preschool, **which in our opinion should be avoided whenever good parenting is possible.** Contrary to common beliefs, little children are not best socialized by other kids; the more persons around them, the fewer meaningful contacts. We found that socialization is not neutral. It tends to be either positive or negative:

Positive or altruistic and principled sociability is firmly linked with the family—with the quantity and quality of self-worth. This is in turn dependent largely on the track of values and experience provided by the family **at least** until the child can reason consistently. In other words, the child who works and eats and plays and has his rest and is read to daily, more with his parents than with his peers, senses that he is part of the family corporation—needed, wanted, depended upon. He is the one who has a sense of self-worth. And when he does enter school, preferably not before 8 to 10, he usually becomes a social leader. He knows where he is going, is independent in values and skills. He largely avoids the dismal pitfalls and social cancer of peer dependency. He is the **productive, self-directed,** citizen our nation badly needs.

Negative, me-first sociability is born from more peer group association and fewer meaningful parental contacts and responsibility experiences in the home during the first 8 to 12 years. The early peer influence generally brings an indifference to family values which defy parent's correction. The child does not yet consistently understand the "why" of parental demands when his peers replace his parents as his models because he is with them more. Research shows that such peer dependency brings loss of (1) self-worth, (2) optimism, (3) respect for parents and (4) trust in peers. What does the child have left to lose? So he does what comes naturally: He adapts to the ways of his agemates because "everybody's doing it," and gives parent values the back of his little hand. And…he has few sound values to pass on to the next generation.

So home, **wherever possible,** is by far the best nest until at least 8 to 10. In a reasonably warm home, adult-child responses, which are the master key to education, will be 50 to 100 times more than the average teacher-child responses in the classroom. Where there is any reasonable doubt about the influence of schools on our children (morality, ridicule, rivalry, denial of religious values, etc.) home schools are usually a highly desirable alternative. Some 35 states permit them by law under various conditions. Other states permit them through court decisions. Home schools nearly always excel regular schools in achievement. Although most of them don't know it, parents are the best teachers for most children at least through ages 10 or 12.

If we are to believe sociologists Frederick Le Play, J.D. Unwin or Carle Zimmerman, we must spend more time with our children in the home, lest our society like Greece and Rome, be lost. The conditions are now identical to theirs. Let's have more loving firmness, less indulgence; more work **with you,** fewer toys; more service for others—the old, poor, infirm—which lead to, and follow, self-worth as children of God. Parents and home, undiluted, usually do this best. **Home-Spun Schools** (Word, 1982) and **The Successful Homeschool Family Handbook** (Thomas Nelson, 1994) will tell how others did it. **Home Style Teaching** (Word, Feb. 1984) will give you new confidence as a teacher whether you teach in home or school, and **Home Built Discipline** (Thomas Nelson, 1987) will help you handle your students. **Better Late Than Early** (Reader's Digest Press, 1975) provides an overview of early childhood research with a guide to the early years, and **School Can Wait** (BYU Press, 1979, 1982) presents exhaustive research on child development and findings indicating the benefits of delaying formal education. A list of Moore publications can be found at http://www.moorefoundation.com/article.php?id=42.

From *How Children Learn* by John Holt[58]

"[Healthy children's learning] leads them out into life in many directions. Each new thing they learn makes them aware of other new things to be learned. Their curiosity grows by what it feeds on. Our task is to keep it well supplied with food, [which] doesn't mean feeding them, or telling them what they have to feed themselves. It means putting within their reach the widest possible variety and quantity of good food—like taking them to a supermarket with no junk food in it (if we can imagine such a thing)...

"Let me sum up what I have been trying to say about the natural learning style of young children. The child is curious. He wants to make sense out of things, find out how things work, gain competence and control over himself and his environment, do what he can see other people doing. He is open, receptive, and perceptive. He does not shut himself off from the strange, confused complicated world around him. He observes it closely and sharply tries to take it all in. He is experimental. He does not merely observe the world around him, but tastes it, touches it, hefts it, bends, breaks it. To find out how reality works, he works on it. He is bold. He is not afraid of making mistakes. And he is patient. He can tolerate an extraordinary amount of uncertainty, confusion, tolerance, and suspense. He does not have to have instant meaning to any situation. He is willing and able to wait for meaning to him—even if it comes very slowly, which it usually does. Children even as young as two want not just to learn about but to be part of our world. They want to become skillful, careful, able to do things and make things as we do. In talking, reading, writing, and many other things they do, children are perfectly able, if not hurried or made ashamed or fearful, to notice and correct most of their own mistakes...

Otto helps a younger homeschool
buddy learn to solder.

"What is lovely about children is that they can make such a production, such a big deal, out of everything, or nothing. From my office I see many families walking down Boylston Street with their little children. The adults plod along, the children twirl, leap, skip, run now to this side and now to that, look for things to step or jump over or walk along or around, climb on anything that can be climbed.

"I never want to be where I cannot see it. All that energy and foolishness, all that curiosity, questions, talk, all those fierce passions, inconsolable sorrows, immoderate joys, seem to many a nuisance to be endured, if not a disease to be cured. To me they are a national asset, a treasure beyond price, more necessary to our health and our very survival than any oil or uranium or—name what you will.

"One day in the Public Garden I see, on a small patch of grass under some trees, a father and a two-year-old girl. The father is lying down; the little girl runs everywhere. What joy to run! Suddenly she stops, looks intently at the ground, bends down, picks something up. A twig! A pebble! She stands up, runs again, sees a pigeon, chases it, suddenly stops and looks up into the sunlit trees, seeing what?—perhaps a squirrel, perhaps a bird, perhaps just the shape and colors of the leaves in the sun. Then she bends down, finds something else, picks it up, examines it. A leaf! Another miracle.

"Gears, twigs, leaves, little children love the world. That is why they are so good at learning about it. For it is love, not tricks and techniques of thought, that lies at the heart of all true learning. Can we bring ourselves to let children learn and grow through that love?

"...All that I am saying in this book can be summed up in two words—Trust Children. Nothing could be more simple or more difficult. Difficult, because to trust children we must trust ourselves—and most of us were taught as children that we could not be trusted. And so we go on treating children as we ourselves were treated, calling this 'reality' or saying bitterly, 'If I could put up with it, they can too.'

"What we have to do is break this long downward cycle of fear and distrust, and trust children as we ourselves were not trusted. To do this will take a long leap of faith—but great rewards await any of us who will take that leap."

Appendix C: Sources for More Information and Materials
Those with an * are highly recommended

Books and CDs

On Homeschooling and Learning in General

*Bach, James. *Secrets of a Buccaneer-Scholar: How Self-Education and the Pursuit of Passion Can Lead to a Lifetime of Success.* 1st ed. New York: Scribner, 2009. Very interesting book written by a young man who was seen as a troublemaker and dropped out of school at sixteen. Four years later he was a manager at Apple Computers.

*Colfax, David, and Micki Colfax. *Homeschooling for Excellence*. New York: Warner Books, 1988. A fascinating description of how this family homeschooled on a rural forty-seven acre homestead, and at the time I read the book, three of their four sons were in or had graduated from Harvard.

Denton, Paula. *The Power of Our Words*. Turner Falls, MA: Northeast Foundation for Children, Inc., 2007. If parents could just learn the way of speaking to children Ms. Denton describes, we would find our whole world far more peaceful.

*Elkind, David. *The Hurried Child*. New York: Perseus Publishing, 2006. Makes a compelling case for letting a child's life unfold at a more natural pace.

*Engelhardt, Anne, and Cheryl Sullivan. *Playful Learning: An Alternative Approach to Preschool*. Schaumburg, IL: La Leche League International, 1986. The principles they found worked with young children have been implemented in preschools across the country. I found that applying them in our home helped enrich our learning while at the same time making life easier. We continued to apply the concepts right on through all our homeschooling years.

Holt, John. *How Children Fail*. New York: Perseus, 1995.

———. *How Children Learn*. New York: Perseus, 1995.

*———. *Learning all the Time*. New York: Perseus, 1990. (quoted at length in Appendix B).

*———. *Teach your Own*. New York: Perseus, 1981, revised and updated by Patrick Farenga as *Teach Your Own: The John Holt Book of Homeschooling*, New York: Perseus, 2003. These two books could be said to have launched the homeschool movement. Then, as now, the prevailing wisdom was that the learner's job is to soak up what the teacher teaches. Holt revolutionized thinking by proposing and offering much support for the idea that the learner would charge full-speed ahead to learn what he needed to learn for his success and happiness, and that our job was mostly to stay out of the way and to help the child access knowledge. One or more of his books are a must-read.

———. *What Do I Do Monday?* Portsmouth, NH: Dutton, 1970; Heinemann, 1995.

Inhelder, Barbel, and Jean Piaget. *The Growth of Logical Thinking: From Childhood to Adolescence*. New York: Basic Books, 1958. So many of our conflicts with children are due to our uninformed expectations of children at their various stages. Understanding these helps us relax, knowing that "to all things there is a season."

*Kohn, Alfie. *Punished by Rewards: The Trouble with Gold Stars, Incentive Plans, A's, Praise, and Other Bribes*. New York: Replica Books, 2001. Before coming across this book, I hadn't realized the harm of rewards as a method of getting children to do as we wish. An important book to read.

Moore, Raymond. *Home Grown Kids.*
    Waco, TX: Word Books, 1981.

*———. *School Can Wait*. Washougal WA:
    Hewitt Research Foundation, 1989.
    Dr. Moore and his wife were fierce advocates
    of delaying school and of having children lead
    real lives within their families. Real work, real
    conversations, and the stable relationships within
    the family were key ingredients in raising a child
    whose intellect and values remained intact.

———. *Better Late Than Early*. New York:
    Reader's Digest Press, 1975, 1982.

Smith, Frank. *Reading Without Nonsense*. 4th ed. New
    York, NY: Teachers College Press, 2005. Our son was a
    late reader and naturally, I worried. Mr. Smith gives a
    new take on reading difficulties, relating them to the
    child not having established a dominant side (sight,
    hand, foot). We applied his techniques, and Thumper
    started reading, though to be honest, I'm not sure if they
    helped his reading or just kept him amused and me
    feeling helpful until he was ready to read. Whichever it
    was doesn't really matter as it took away any pressure
    and reading proceeded smoothly after that.

*Spigel, Laurie Block. *Education Uncensored: A Guide
    for the Aspiring, the Foolhardy and the Disillusioned*.
    New York: HomeschoolNYC, 2009. Mrs. Spigel tells
    her story of challenges and victories and how she
    evolved into a homeschooler after her son was
    expelled from elementary school. With many practical

ideas for teaching various subjects, I especially liked her chapter giving examples of comprehensive curricula each designed around a particular interest, horses, art, fairy tales, herbs, to name a few.

Thoreau, Henry, David, *Walden; Or, Life in the Woods*. Reprint ed. Castle, NJ: Castle Books, 2007. Thoreau makes a good case for the importance of hands-on, practical education as compared to book learning.

On Special Education and ADD

I must admit I have only read the first book below and am not at all versed on special education other than what I saw when I substitute taught some special education classes last year. I saw adolescent boys in high school acting up because nothing they were learning had any relevance to them and meanwhile the children who needed help were in far over their heads. Also, mothers have told me that their children had no problems with behavior and focus once they were out of the confines of the school environment. These were enough to convince me that any parent would be wise to examine other alternatives than what schools provide. These books are offered as a place for the concerned parent to start looking for answers.

Amen, Daniel G. *Healing ADD*. New York: The Berkley Publishing Group, 2001.

Armstrong, Thomas. *The Myth of the A.D.D. Child: 50 Ways to Improve Your Child's Behavior and Attention Span without Drugs, Labels, or Coercion*. New York: Penguin Books, 1995.

———. *Seven Kinds of Smart: Identifying and Developing Your Multiple Intelligences.* New York: Penguin Books, 1999.

Goddard, Sally. *Reflexes, Learning and Behavior: A Window into the Child's Mind.* Eugene, OR: Fern Ridge Press, 2005.

———. *The Well Balanced Child: Movement and Early Learning.* 2nd ed. Hawthorne, NJ: Hawthorne Press. 2006.

———. *A Teacher's Window Into the Child's Mind.* Eugene, OR: Fern Ridge Press, 1996.

Granger, Bill. *The Magic Feather: The Truth about Special Education.* 1st ed. New York: E. P. Dutton, 1986.

Pauc, Robin. *The Learning Disability Myth: Understanding and Overcoming Your Child's Diagnosis of Dyspraxia, Tourette's Syndrome of Childhood, ADD, ADHD or OCD.* New York: Virgin Books, 2006.

Strydom, Jan, and Susan Du Plessis. *The Myth of ADHD and Other Learning Disabilities.* Lafayette, LA: Huntington House Publishers, 2001.

On Teens and College

Cohen, Cafi. *Homeschoolers' College Admissions Handbook.* illustrated ed. New York: Three Rivers Press, 2000.

———. *Homeschoolers' College Admissions Handbook: Preparing Your 12- to 18-Year-Old for a Smooth Transition.* illustrated ed. Eugene. OR: Three Rivers Press,2000. College was never an issue for us as

Thumper was fine with the possibility of going to the community college here and transferring to the University of Hawaii later if he wanted to. But for parents whose children are headed straight for selective colleges, this book can be a big help.

Llewellyn, Grace. *Real Lives: Eleven Teenagers Who Don't Go to School Tell Their Own Stories*. Eugene, OR: Lowry House Publishers, 2005.

*————. *The Teenage Liberation Handbook: How to Quit School and Get a Real Life and Education*. Eugene, OR: Lowry House Publishers, 1998. Teen years are usually the time when homeschooling parents start feeling they ought to send their kids to school. (Interestingly, parents of schooled children seem to become more worried about schools at the same time.) These two books demonstrate that homeschooled children can do just fine without school even in their teen years.

On Schools Both Alternative and Traditional

*Gatto, John Taylor. *Dumbing Us Down: The Hidden Curriculum of Compulsory Schooling*. 2nd ed. Gabriola Island, BC Canada: New Society Publishers, 2002. Gatto was a school teacher for thirty years and New York State Teacher of the Year. This book is a classic in homeschool literature and a must-read to get an insider's description of our school system. The list of the ten things an educated person must know are a great place to start with designing a curriculum or evaluating a packaged one.

———. *The Exhausted School: Bending the Bars of Traditional Education.* 2nd ed. Berkeley, CA: Berkeley Hills Books, 2002.

———. *A Schooling Is Not an Education.* Audio cassette or CD. Pathway Book Services, 2001. http://www.johntaylorgatto.com/index.htm.

———. *What Is An Education?* Audio cassette or CD. Pathway Book Services, 2001. http://www.johntaylorgatto.com/index.htm.

———. *The Seven-Lesson Schoolteacher* (audio cassette or CD). Pathway Book Services, 2001. http://www.johntaylorgatto.com/index.htm.

*———. *Weapons of Mass Instruction: A Schoolteacher's Journey through the Dark World of Compulsory Schooling.* Gabriola Island, BC Canada: New Society Publishers, 2010. Mr. Gatto continues to be an articulate and passionate advocate for children and for improving how we educate them.

*Greenberg, Daniel. *Free at Last.* Framingham, MA: Sudbury Valley School Press, 1995. Written about an alternative school that uses child-centered curricula, the ideas in this are equally applicable to homeschooling. My favorite chapter is one about the boy who fished and seemed to do nothing else. Of course the parents fretted—wouldn't you? As Mr. Greenberg says in this book, "We felt that the only learning that ever counts in life happens when the learners have thrown themselves into a subject on

their own, without coaxing, or bribing, or pressure"
Read the book to see how it turns out for them. You've
read how it turned out for our boy who rollerbladed!

Loewen, James W. *Lies My Teacher Told Me: Everything
Your American Textbook Got Wrong.* New York: The
New Press, 1995. I felt like I was from another country
learning American History for the first time. The author
exposes the political agenda of our history books and
the interconnectedness between the various textbook
publishers. If you want the full picture of our history (or
any other subject, for that matter), he urges readers
to go to the original sources rather than textbooks.

On Parenting

Homeschooling is obviously a parenting choice and how
we parent will have profound influence on our success as
homeschoolers. Here are some important books for any
parent in general but for homeschoolers in particular.

*Aldort, Naomi. *Raising Our Children, Raising Ourselves.*
Eastsound, Washington: Naomi Aldort, PhD, 2006.

——.*Trusting Our Children, Trusting Ourselves* (different than
the book). Six keynote speeches given by Ms. Aldort
covering most parenting issues. A comprehensive set of
seven CDs, these would be very helpful to parents who
want to raise their children to be self-directed adults. Ms.
Aldort offers books, lectures, online, and phone help and
more via her web site: http://www.naomialdort.com/.

*Berends, Polly Berrien. *Whole Child/Whole Parent.* rev. ed.
New York: HarperCollins. 1997. I read my first copy so

many times that it fell apart, and I had to buy another. Practical and inspirational, it's my favorite parenting book, and I'd like to add a row of *s to express how highly I recommend it. Ms. Berends captures the essence of the noblest aims of parenting. Practical advice, yes, but it is the appeal to our highest selves as well that points us in the direction of being the best parent and the best person we can be.

*Faber, Adele, and Elaine Mazlish. *How to Talk So Kids Will Listen & Listen So Kids Will Talk.* Rev ed. Eugene Oregon: Three Rivers Press, 2003. Another book I would not parent without. Based on the teachings of Dr. Ginott, this and the books below are supremely practical books. I posted a chart of solutions mentioned in this book in my bathroom and whenever things got testy with our son, I'd tell him I had to use the toilet. I'd excuse myself and while in the bathroom, I'd choose a solution, and if the first one didn't work, I'd go back to the toilet. I always found something that worked and our lives were far more harmonious than they'd have been without this book.

*———. *Liberated Parents, Liberated Children: Your Guide to a Happier Family.* New York: Avon Books, Inc., 1990. Factual and anecdotal, this book makes very clear how much difference a mood or attitude can make in child-rearing. This was the book that introduced me to the work of Dr. Ginott, and opened my eyes to a different way of parenting—one that respects the dignity of the child without being permissive. After reading it, I sought out everything written by him or based on his works.

*———. *Siblings Without Rivalry: How to Help Your Children Live Together So You Can Live Too*. New York: Avon Books, 1987, 1998. Indispensable if your child has siblings or friends! Our son grew up as an only child, but we always had a houseful of children. I felt it was best for all the children that I took care of not to play favorites, so I treated all children as if they were mine. Most of the time I was able to keep the fun and peace in these interactions using tips from this book.

*Ginott, Haim G. *Between Parent and Child*. Rev ed. Eugene, OR: Three Rivers Press, 2003.

*———. *Between Parent and Teenager*. New York: Avon Books, 1988. Ginott's books are groundbreaking with their emphasis on respect and two-way communication with children. I give much credit to these books for the fact that we never had any teenage rebellion problems. Parents who are having difficulty understanding or talking with their adolescents or teens will find this book a life-changer if they are open to its message.

*Hymes, James L. Jr. *The Child Under Six*. New York: Prentice Hall, 1971. This is a man who truly understands the behavior of young children. His description of "naughty but nice" sums it up—some behaviors are not what we'd wish but are exactly what the child should be doing at a particular developmental stage (like how toddlers want to "get into everything.") He wisely writes that we may as well relax in the face of the inevitable because they will outgrow that behavior just as they do diapers. Parents and children will all be happier if we let go of our ideas

that if we don't scold, punish, and cajole, our children
will never stop the behavior we think needs fixing

Leach, Penelope. *The Child Care Encyclopedia.*
New York: Knopf, 1984.

*————. *Your Baby and Child: From Birth to Age Five.* 3rd ed.
New York: Alfred A. Knopf, 1997, 2010. This and *Whole
Child/Whole Parent* cited earlier are my standard baby
shower gifts. The introductions to the sections and the
photos are precious. She is both poetic and practical,
making this a book to read for sheer enjoyment and
to refer to for answers to particular questions.

*Linthorst, Ann. *A Gift of Love: Marriage as a Spiritual
Journey.* Orange, CA: PAGL Press, 1979. This is part of
my standard wedding gift package. Based on the
work of psychiatrist, Thomas Hora, this book is non-
denominational, with lots of Christian and other quotes
from spiritual and religious leaders, and appropriate
for all readers, religious or spiritual or neither. The
principles she shares are helpful in any relationship.

*————. *Mothering as a Spiritual Journey: Learning to Let
God Nurture Your Children and You Along with Them.*
New York: Crossroad Pub Co., 1993. While loaded
with down-to-earth advice and stories, this book is
all about the transcendental aspects of parenting,
about understanding, integrity, and our divine nature.
After reading this book, I came away with a far higher
appreciation of mothering and its potential for good,
not only in my family but in the world at-large.

Web Sites

On Homeschooling in General

- A–Z Home's Cool. http://homeschooling.gomilpitas. com/. Ann Zeise is the first place to go to research any particular topic pertaining to homeschooling.

- About.com. "Homeschooling." http:// homeschooling.about.com/

- ———. "Homeschooling Basics (101)." http://homeschooling.about.com/od/ gettingstarted/p/homeschool101.htm.

- Clonlara School. http://www.clonlara.org/. Provides variety of services for all ages, from simple materials up to a custom curriculum tailored for your child, diplomas, and handling of DOE representatives, principals and such in your school district. This is a source for a curriculum designed and administrated specifically for your child. I have visited their campus, spoken with their staff, and had some contact with them throughout the years. I was impressed with their professionalism and feel their services fill an important niche for some families.

- *Home Education Magazine.* http://www. homeedmag.com/. This magazine was my lifeline when few people were homeschooling. Having a magazine come in my mailbox (now maybe it would be my e-mail box) kept reminding me of what I was doing and why and gave me ideas and a sense of an informed community when here we were all inexperienced in any of this. A subscription to this magazine will be a steady source of information and inspiration.

- Learning Without Schooling. http://www.patfarenga. com/. The magazine, Learning Without Schooling, was another of my lifelines for information and support in our choice to unschool. While the print magazine has been discontinued, Pat continues to promote the philosophy, and his web site is a treasure trove of information.

- Moore Homeschooling. http://www. moorefoundation.com/. Again, one of my important mentors with much well-documented research and assistance with programs and materials.

- The Odysseus Group. "John Taylor Gatto." http:// www.johntaylorgatto.com. You will be astonished by the information here about our public school system.

- Sonia Story Consulting. "Move, Play, Thrive!" http://www.moveplaythrive.com. Story promotes using interventions based on specific childhood reflex movements.

A weekly Lego Club building session.

Great sites for research on socialization in school compared to homeschooled

- http://www.ontariohomeschool.org/socialization.shtml

- http://www.nheri.org/Research-Facts-on-Homeschooling.html

- And this one for research on academics and demographics: http://www.nheri.org/Latest/Homeschooling-Across-America-Academic-Achievement-and-Demographic-Characteristics.html

- For parents involved in custody issues, homeschoolers can contact other homeschoolers for information about homeschooling attorneys and experts and exchange information about handling custody disputes as a result of homeschooling: http://groups.yahoo.com/group/AHSA-USA_Homeschooling_and_Custody/

Articles and News Stories

- Aldort, Naomi, "Living and Learning With Children." *Life Learning Magazine* (March/April 2002). In this first issue, now out of print, Ms. Aldort writes about the value of play and the difficulty of our knowing what the child is really learning from any given situation, whether deemed "educational" or not. Full article quoted at HomeschoolingWhyandHow.com

- Kantrowitz, Barbara, and Pat Wingert. "What Makes a High School Great?" *Newsweek*, (May 8, 2006). http://www.newsweek.com/id/34509. Article gives traits uncannily like homeschooling.

- Morford, Mark. "American Kids, Dumber than Dirt." *SF Gate* (October 24, 2007). http://www.sfgate.com/cgi-bin/article.cgi?f=/g/a/2007/10/24/notes102407.DTL.

- "Testing Parents." October 3, 2007. John Fink Editorial on KHNL TV and now in written form on http://www.khnl.com

Sources for Curricula

- Clonlara School. http://www.clonlara.org/. This is a source for a curriculum designed and administrated just for your child. I have visited their campus, spoken with their teachers, and had some contact with them throughout the years and feel their services fill an important niche for some families.

- Global Student Network. "Online Homeschool Curriculum." http://www.globalstudentnetwork. com/homeschool/index.php. Online curriculum for grades two through twelve.

- Home School Inc. "HomeSchool Reviews." http://www.homeschoolreviews.com/default. aspx. For more information than you'll likely want on more curricula than you'll ever need.

- Homeschool Buyers Club. https://www. homeschoolbuyersco-op.org/. Founded to level the playing field by creating the world's largest purchasing cooperative for homeschoolers.

- The Homeschool Curriculum Shop. http:// www.homeschoolcurriculumshop.com/ store.html. A one-stop shop for various curricula, both secular and religious.

- The Khan Academy. http://www. Khanacademy. com. A library of over 2,100 educational videos covering math, science, humanities, economics, history, test preparation, and more. Each is a ten- to fifteen-minute self-paced lesson. This just might be the future of education both in schools and for homeschoolers.

Some Just Plain Interesting Sites

- Babuata, Leo. "Education Needs to Be Turned on Its Head." *Zenhabits*, August 2009. http:// zenhabits.net/2009/08/education-needs-to-be-turned-on-its-head/. The author, a truly fascinating person, father of six, and married to a teacher, discusses what is wrong with the current model of education and what can be done about it.

- Edutopia. "Big Thinkers: Jon Young on Lessons from Nature." http://www.edutopia.org/jon-young. Jon Young cofounder of the Wilderness Awareness School in 1983, is a tracker and advocate of the importance of spending regular time in nature. On the video he speaks about our children having a "nature-deficit disorder."

- Sawaya, Nathan. "The Art of the Brick." http:// www.brickartist.com/gallery.html. Former attorney, Nathan Sawaya, is now a Lego artist and a great example of a schooled student who did everything he was "supposed to"—he became an attorney—but he was unhappy. He became a famous and well-paid Lego artist and loves it.

- TED. "Ken Robinson Says Schools Kill Creativity." February 2006, http://www.ted.com/talks/ken_robinson_says_schools_kill_creativity.html.
- ———. "Why Teaching is Not Like Making Motor Cars."
- http://www.cnn.com/2010/OPINION/03/17/ted.ken.robinson/index.html?hpt=C1

These exceedingly informative and entertaining talks will make you laugh and make you think.

Acknowledgments

Thank you to my husband, Jordan, for trusting me as I researched, experimented, and ended up homeschooling our son for so long. He is my can-do man, and we could not have done all we did without his support; to our son, Thumper, for his companionship, enthusiasm, and, most of all, his inspiration—he came to us as our child, but he was also our best teacher. I'm grateful for the excellent suggestions he made to improve this book; to my parents and brothers for their loving attention to Thumper even when they feared I was ruining his life. I am happy that they were all able to see that their fears were unfounded.

Thank you to those who helped with this book: Ken Pinsky, friend, cocreator of several homeschool newsletters, seminars, and activities, and an editor of this book; Karen Bacon; Paul Wood; Dan Millman; and Larry Koss; to all the authors of all the articles and books I read that helped me keep the faith—especially *The Moore Foundation*, *Home Education Magazine* and *Growing Without Schooling*. The latter two published articles I wrote, allowing me to return the favor by helping other homeschoolers; to all the Maui homeschoolers with whom we shared so many great times and who gave their energy to our support group, HAPPY (Homeschool Adventures: Program for Parents and Youngsters). Thanks to good friend Melisa Swarm, and her son, Otto, who helped gather many of the photos and permissions in the book. Special thanks to my father for always having faith in me, and for loving me, my husband, and Thumper unconditionally. Knowing I had him in my corner as my champion helped me in more ways than I can name.

Lastly, I am grateful for our son and all the children, both in school and homeschooled, who shared our homes and lives. They brought us so much happiness, and we are still involved with many of them. We learned a great deal from them about what really matters in life.

Mahalo and Aloha,

Gail (Peterson) Nagasako

Maui, Hawaii

Thumper, Gail, and Jordan

Author's Notes and Biography

I grew up in Ann Arbor, home of the University of Michigan. I spent many weekends and summers hanging out on campus and eventually went to college there, graduating with honors and a teacher's certificate. I learned many things from that vibrant university town atmosphere, the most important of which was respect for diversity and other points of view. This was perhaps predictive of how I happened to take a novel approach to the education of our son.

After graduation I moved to Hawaii. I had fallen in love with the islands in third grade when our teacher came back from her honeymoon there and shared her experiences with us. I taught sixth grade, did some substitute teaching in high schools, and went on to become a counselor and a freelance writer. I always expected to have children and assumed they would go to public schools and a good university like I did. The many forks in our road that led to us homeschooling are described in the article in Chapter One, "I Never Set Out to Be a Homeschooler."

I founded a support group for homeschoolers, and later an alternative school. I wrote articles for local newsletters, newspapers, and national magazines, and compiled a booklet on homeschooling, which the Hawaii State Library System reprinted, placing twenty copies in their system. I counseled parents who found me online or were referred to me by the county schools.

After our son moved on from homeschooling into creating his own business (http://hifocused.com/), I went back to substitute teaching. I was dumbfounded with what I saw, and it confirmed what I had been hearing from distraught parents all along—school was too often no place for children. I kept fielding phone calls and finally realized that I had to share more broadly what I had learned about homeschooling and how to do it. Thus, this book was born.

Now, I haven't said much about my husband, Jordan, and I'd like to share with you his story as he has sketched it out for me.

Jordan had a very different experience growing up in Hawaii. He was, in his words, "wild," and he struggled in the confines of school, often skipping to go surfing. He muddled through and managed to complete three years of college. After working in his family's supermarket, he started a fish wholesale business and became a very successful businessman. He came to parenthood with the same expectations as I did but also with the hope that his son would achieve what he did not—success in school and a good education.

We were in complete agreement about flying off to Philadelphia to a weeklong class to teach us how to maximize the potential of any children we might have in the future. When our son was born, we both participated in the program enthusiastically with him. This worked for a while, and then came one of many forks in our educational path.

Jordan wasn't at all sure that homeschooling was the right path, but since I had done my homework and was determined to use our son's inner spark to drive his education, Jordan went along with it. Soon he started seeing the benefits. He saw our son learning real-world lessons, responsibility, and communication skills beyond his years. His concern about socialization vanished as he saw Thumper with a diverse group of friends, both schooled and homeschooled.

We could share our family values and make sure our son got plenty of wholesome food, fresh air, sufficient sleep, and exercise doing the many activities we all enjoyed. We could travel, camp, and surf when other children were in school and their parents working. Jordan had more time to share his knowledge and skills with his son without having to compete with school and homework.

We are happy we were able to give our son a rich, full childhood, and when he was ready for academics he learned them quickly and easily at home because he was ready, he had his own purpose for doing so, and he didn't have the distractions omnipresent in school classrooms.

Whether you end up homeschooling for a month, a year, or for all of the school years, you will never regret those extra moments you were able to share with your children. We sure don't!

Endnotes

1. U.S. Department of Education, "U.S. Education Secretary Announces Budget That Advances Reform While Cutting Waste," news release, May 7, 2009, http://www.ed.gov/news/pressreleases/2009/05/05072009a.html.

2. CollegeBoard, "2009–10 College Prices," http://www.collegeboard.com/student/pay/add-it-up/4494.html.

3. Brian Wingfield and Daniel Indiviglio, "The Most Expensive U.S. Colleges," Forbes, February 3, 2009, http://www.forbes.com/2009/02/03/most-expensive-colleges-business-0203_colleges.html.

4. Ann Zeise, "Numbers of Homeschoolers in USA," A to Z Home's Cool, http://homeschooling.gomilpitas.com/weblinks/numbers.htm.

5. Ann Zeise, "S.A.T. and Other College Entrance Tests," A to Z Home's Cool, http://homeschooling.gomilpitas.com/olderkids/CollegeTests.htm.

6. Ann Zeise, "Numbers of Homeschoolers in USA," A to Z Home's Cool, http://homeschooling.gomilpitas.com/weblinks/numbers.htm.

7. John Taylor Gatto, A Map, A Mirror and a Wristwatch, SKOLE: The Journal of Alternative Education, v11 n2 p48-69 Sum 1994   For more articles and speeches by Gatto, go to http://www.johntaylorgatto.com/. Also see his "Teacher of the Year Acceptance Speech," January 31, 1990, www.afhe.org/resources/articles/gatto_teacher_of_year_speech_1990.pdf.

8. "A Synopsis" was written to present the material from the book School Can Wait. Raymond S. Moore et al., School Can Wait. (Provo, UT: BYU Press, 1979, 1982). Updated by Kathie Kordenbrock, daughter of Dr. Moore ©April 21, 2010 (Full Text is in Appendix B). For a list of other articles Moore published, please go to http://www.moorefoundation.com/article.php?id=42. http://www.moorefoundation.com/article.php?id=42.

9. C. George Boeree, "Jean Piaget and Cognitive Development," http://webspace.ship.edu/cgboer/genpsypiaget.html.

10. Kathleen Nadeau, "Gender Issues in the Diagnosis and Treatment of ADHD: An Interview with Kathleen Nadeau, PhD." http://www.athealth.com/Practitioner/particles/interview_nadeau.html.

11. The Institutes for the Achievement of Human Potential, http://www.iahp.org/.

12. The Institutes for the Achievement of Human Potential, "How to Multiply Your Baby's Intelligence Course," http://www.iahp.org/How-T.215.0.html.

13. Shunryu Suzuki, *Zen Mind, Beginner's Mind,* New Ed ed. (New York and Tokyo: John Weatherhill, Inc., 1973).

14. For a more detailed description of the research regarding delaying school, see the "Synopsis" by Dr. Raymond Moore in appendix B and the books listed in appendix C.

15. http://www.test-guide.com/ged-scores.html

16. Vert is short for vertical and describes a U shaped ramp that has anywhere from six inches to several feet of vertical wall at the top of the U.

17. See Thumper's web sites for more information: http://hifocused.com/; and http://www.thumpernagasako.com/.

18. Names have been changed to protect the innocent and the guilty. Schools in your area may not be as bad as this (though they might be worse), but you might want to ask your children to read this account and tell you if any of these antics go on in their classes.

19. Ann Zeise, "S.A.T. and Other College Entrance Tests," A to Z Home's Cool, http://homeschooling. gomilpitas.com/olderkids/CollegeTests.htm.

20. Michelle Baron, "Socialization and the Homeschooled Student," Homeschool Association of California, http://www.education.com/reference/article/ Ref_Socialization/; The Ontario Federation of Teaching Parents, "Socialization of homeschooled children," http:// www.ontariohomeschool.org/socialization.shtml.

21. John Loeffler, "The Myth of Socialization," Steel on Steel, http://www.steelonsteel.com/articles/myth_socialization. html; *Phyllis Schlafly*, "Is Socialization a Problem for Homeschoolers?" *The Moral Liberal*, (January 26, 2010), http://www.themoralliberal.com/2010/01/26/is-socialization-a-problem-for-homeschoolers-phyllis-schlafly/.

22. Kristi Monson and Arthur Schoenstadt, "Ritalin Side Effects," eMedTV, http://adhd.emedtv. com/ritalin/ritalin-side-effects.html.

23. "A Synopsis" . Moore see end note 8 for details

24. Allen Carlson, "How Homeschooling Strengthens Families," The Howard Center, (April 17, 1998), http:// www.profam.org/docs/acc/thc_acc_hhssf.htm.

25. Additionally, regulations can be found online. Ann Zeise, "Regional and World Wide Homeschooling," A to Z Home's Cool, http://homeschooling. gomilpitas.com/regional/Region.htm.

26. Anne Zeise, "S.A.T. and Other College Entrance Tests," A to Z Home's Cool, http://homeschooling. gomilpitas.com/olderkids/CollegeTests.htm.

27. "A Synopsis" see endnote 8 for details.

28. For a complete list of famous people who were homeschooled some or all of their younger years, please visit http://www.famoushomeschoolers.net/index.html.

29. Abundant support for this approach is in the book *School Can Wait* by Dr. Raymond Moore. Hewitt Research Foundation (August 1989).

30. For some excellent examples of interest-based comprehensive curricula, please see Laurie Spigel Block, *Education Uncensored: A Guide for the Aspiring, the Foolhardy and the Disillusioned* (New York: Homeschool NYC, 2009).

31. Ms. vos Savant is listed in the Guinness Book of World Records for "Highest IQ." "About Marilyn," http://www.marilynvossavant.com/bio.html.

32. ©1998 Marilyn vos Savant. Initially published in Parade Magazine. All rights reserved

33. Albert Einstein. Quotes.net (April 9, 2010), http://www.quotes.net/quote/9260.

34. Ann Zeise, "S.A.T. and Other College Entrance Tests," A to Z Home's Cool, http://homeschooling.gomilpitas.com/olderkids/CollegeTests.htm.

35. For more famous college drop-outs, go to http://www.collegedropoutshalloffame.com/j.htm;

36. also an article "Billionaire College Dropouts," http://www.rediff.com/money/2005/sep/15sld1.htm.

37. Hawaii's Windows of Opportunity is an example of this type of service. For more information, visit http://woohawaii.com/packages.php.

38. For a highly entertaining talk on the overemphasis on academics in our schools, watch Ken Robinson's talk at http://www.ted.com/talks/lang/eng/ken_robinson_says_schools_kill_creativity.html.

39. *The LINK Homeschool Newspaper* 5, no. 3,
    2002, http://www.homeschoolnewslink.com/
    homeschool/articles/vol5iss3/ICry_v5i3.htm.

40. The basis for this approach came from Engelhardt
    and Sullivan, *Playful Learning: an Alternative
    Approach to Preschool* (Schaumburg, IL :La
    Leche League International,1986). I found that
    the techniques were workable at all ages.

41. Milk covers are the round caps used on old milk and juice
    bottles. Here in Hawaii, and perhaps in some other states,
    children developed a game where they could win milk
    covers from others, and special designs were also bought,
    sold, and traded. The game was popular when my
    husband was a boy and again when our son was a boy.

42. Many homeschooling parents ignore all of the
    homeschooling regulations and simply go about
    the business of living their lives and educating their
    children. Generally, this is due to either a desire to not
    be bothered with red tape and/or a political stance
    that the government has no business involving itself
    in the lives and education of a family. These families
    do have a constitutional basis for this, but that issue
    is beyond the scope of this book. This section is for
    those who choose to comply with the regulations.

43. Hawaii Administrative Rules, "Compulsory Attendance
    Exceptions," sec. 8-12-13, http://lilinote.k12.hi.us/PUBLIC/
    ADMINR1.NSF/85255a0a0010ae82852555340060479d/a4
    9d572fb0811e390a25675a00750641?OpenDocument.

44. "Responsibility," (New York: The Readers
    Digest Association, Inc., 1996). -

45. Hawaii Administrative Rules, "Compulsory Attendance
    Exceptions," sec. 8-12-14, http://lilinote.k12.hi.us/PUBLIC/
    ADMINR1.NSF/85255a0a0010ae82852555340060479d/a4
    9d572fb0811e390a25675a00750641?OpenDocument.

46. Hawaii Administrative Rules, "Compulsory Attendance Exceptions," sec. 8-12-15, http://lilinote.k12.hi.us/ PUBLIC/ADMINR1.NSF/85255a0a0010ae828525 55340060479d/a49d572fb0811e390a25675a00 750641?OpenDocument; emphasis mine.

47. John Holt,*Teach Your Own* , (New York: Dell Publishing Co., Inc,, 1981).

48. You can also download these forms from http:// www.homeschoolingwhyandhow.com.

49. You can find information online at About.com. Beverly Hernandez, "Homeschool Support Groups by State," About.com, http://homeschooling.about. com/od/supportgroupsbystate/a/sgusa.htm.

50. L. Ron Hubbard, *The Learning Book*, (Copenhagenn K, Denmark: New Era Publications International, 1984).

51. Ibid.

52. Ibid.

53. Ibid.

54. "Death of Raymond Moore," Moore Academy, http:// www.moorefoundation.com/article.php?id=23.

55. "John Holt and Growing Without Schooling," http://www.holtgws.com/johnholtpage.html.

56. "A Synopsis" see endnote 8 for details.

57. New York: Perseus, 1995.

58. Copyright © 1995 John Holt. Reprinted by permission of Da Capo Press, a member of the Perseus Books Group.